Immigrant
iN PERiL

Immigrant
iN PERiL

Carl Tangeman's Heroic Journey Across America
1847-1848

CHERYL D. CLAY

Immagrant in Peril
Carl Tangeman's Heroic Journey Across America 1847-1848

Cover design, book design and layout by Jim L. Friesen

Library of Congress Control Number: 2016933295

International Standard Book Number: 978-0-9971515-0-3

Printed in the United States of America by Mennonite Press, Inc., Newton, Kansas. www.MennonitePress.com

Dedication

This book is dedicated to my adventurous grandchildren: Wolf, Maren, Ephram, Heidi, Noa and Fred who are also direct descendents of Carl Heinrich Tangeman.

Contents

Introduction

I am truly pleased and honored to have been asked to write the introduction to this book due to the fact the author and I are great-great granddaughter and great-granddaughter, respectively, of Carl Heinrich Tangeman whose story unfolds in the following pages.

The background of the story is written with respect to the social, economic and political situation in the 1800s both in Europe and the United States. Actual documents detailing milestone events in Carl's life are in the possession of family, and, therefore, use of dates, letters, legal papers and other happenings are incorporated into the story.

There is probably not a one of us who has not heard stories of older or deceased relatives, the "old days" and the "old country." Who has not wondered how their forefathers lived in earlier centuries? Where did they live in the world? What work did they pursue? What were the living conditions of most families? How large were families? What were the biggest challenges? How did economic and political conditions affect their lives? Was there hope for a good life in the future? What made them decide to immigrate despite the risk of a dangerous voyage? All these questions need to be answered when we ask, "Who was Carl Heinrich Tangeman?"

The impetus for this book was the author's interest in genealogy and her desire to write this story for her grandchildren so they might learn about their forefather. The choice of this fictionalized biography with an easy storyline was penned in a way that she hoped would be enjoyable to read and learn about

Carl Heinrich Tangeman, an actual relative. These great-great-great-great grandchildren will know that Carl survived a long, dangerous, sad and discouraging journey from Prussia to the New World. His perseverance, hope and vision for a better life in the United States drove him on in times of despair.

Thus, Carl Heinrich Tangeman reigns as the patriarch of the eventual Kansas branch of the Tangeman Family. In 2015, his known and recorded descendants number 1275. What a legacy! No doubt Carl would be amazed by how his family has grown, prospered and contributed to the better life he sought over 150 years ago.

It is hoped that pride and appreciation for past family accomplishments will challenge future generations to achieve their goals, seek adventure, remain industrious and trustworthy, become leaders, uphold moral values and always have faith in God.

Peg Tangeman Wickersham
Tangeman Family Historian
October 5, 2015

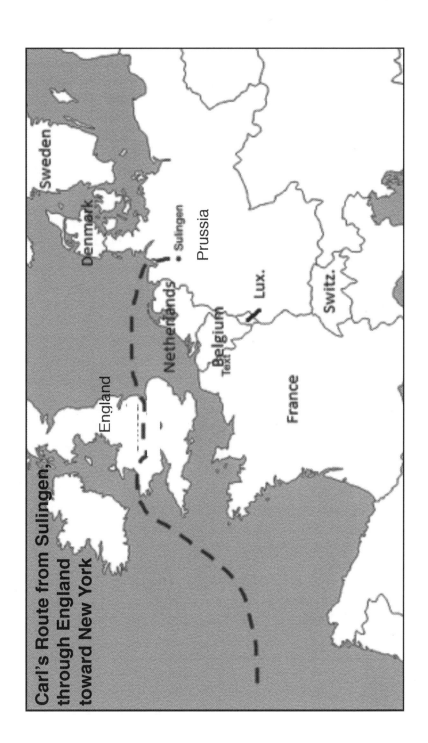

Carl's Route from Sulingen, through England toward New York

Sweden

Denmark

Sulingen

Prussia

Netherlands

England

Belgium

Lux.

Switz.

France

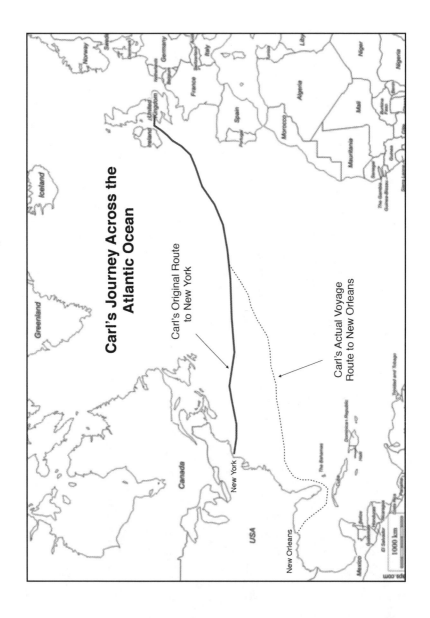

Carl's Journey Across the Atlantic Ocean

Carl's Original Route to New York

Carl's Actual Voyage Route to New Orleans

Carl's Journey Across the U.S., New Orleans, Louisiana to New York City and back to Cincinnati, Ohio & Route of George and Wilhelm from New York City to Cincinnati, Ohio, 1847-48

Prologue

Carl and Elizabeth Tangemann left their home in Sulingen, Hannover, Prussia in 1847 bound for New York. Poor crops for the previous two years had brought starvation to northern Europe. When war broke out with the Danes and revolutionary upheaval erupted across the continent in 1847, the young couple was pushed to risk their lives for a better chance to survive in America. News of jobs and opportunity from Carl's brothers, George and Wilhelm, who had emigrated the previous year, also pulled them toward America.

With the blessings of their families, the Tangemanns boarded a packet ship in Liverpool, England to cross the fearsome Atlantic Ocean. They joined over 1.7 million European emigrants with similar motives who reached American shores in the 1840s. America offered a refuge from war and an escape from starvation. This "common" story of 19th century immigration struggles is laced with uncommonly heroic adventures as Carl is transformed from Prussian villager to American pioneer.

Chapter 1
Farewell

FAREWELL LETTER FROM FRIEDRICH TANGEMANN,
CARL'S FATHER, IN SULINGEN, HANNOVER, PRUSSIA TO
CARL AND ELIZABETH TANGEMANN* IN BRAKE
ON THE WESER RIVER

The family name was spelled Tangemann in Prussia. It was changed to the Americanized spelling of Tangeman with one "n" in the United States.

August 28, 1847
Brake (on the Weser River), Hannover, Prussia
c/o Herr Weber

Dear Children,
Gladly would I like to have seen you and spoken to you again, especially when I think that it will be the last time in this life. But I cannot make the load easier for you, and I am afraid that it would not be good for me. Go courageously your path, trust in God, and live happy if it is so ordained by God to give you a better life. What(ever) will happen. I will remember you as long as I live, and remember you in my prayers. I say an eternal "farewell" to you....

...*Farewell, your father, F. T. (Friedrich Tangemann)*
Sulingen, Hannover, Prussia*

*This letter was translated from German and is quoted verbatim as it was recorded in English in The Carl Heinrich Tangeman Genealogy, 1821-1971, *1971.*

Sulingen, Hannover, Prussia in March, 1847

In *slunken* steps, a tawny gray wolf slid between gaping door and splintered jam of the disheveled hut, and faded away, off the sagging porch into dark and dusky forest. Had the captain heard whispered movements of other heads, torsos or tails slip away, or merely a raw slash of wind? His eyes darted from tumbledown shack to its frame of icy trunks and back again. These predators hunted in packs.

Carl directed nine soldiers of his local *Sandstrom* militia detail to ease forward, while gripping the magazine of his own rifle. Wolves were uncommon in the rolling countryside of northern Prussian plains. But this winter brought starvation to more living creatures, humans and animals, wild and tame. Colder than usual, rainier than last year, low-lying river towns were inundated by rain off and on during 1847, like 1846 and 1845. Downpours had reduced rye and wheat to dangerously poor harvests, and potatoes rotted from blight.

Darkness hid the disorderly hovel's inhabitants from sight, but not their smell. Carl coughed to clear his nose of the stench of bodies left too long alone. There was barely enough daylight to see inside the hut, a blessing to those tasked to bury the dead. The ground was partly frozen, partly water-logged from rain. But it gave way to shovels thrust deep enough to hollow out the family's final rest.

On the trek back to Sulingen, Otto, second in command of the local militia unit, lamented, "Poor things. 'Twas a horrible way to die."

"Parents and five *kinder*. They moved here last summer from further east," added a fellow soldier.

Carl addressed his nine fellow peacekeepers, "What we witnessed in the forest hut was haunting, especially the marks of the wolf. It could start a panic back in the village. May I ask you not to talk about what we just saw and buried?"

"*Ja, ja*. That is fine if we keep this to ourselves," replied Otto. He spoke for the company of local militia who nodded their agreement as they tramped back home in darkness and grave silence.

Sulingen, Hannover, Prussia in April, 1847

Tinkling bells and whistles from the wooden bridge announced a rickety, colorful, horse-drawn wagon lurching toward the center of town. Herr Schultz, a tall, lanky shipping agent with a straggly, dark beard had come from Bremerhaven to recruit emigrants in the Sulingen area. He waved to the townspeople, his woolen day coat draped haphazardly over his shoulders.

"Carl, Carl, the shipping agent is here," called Elizabeth urgently to her husband. She quickly secured her month-old infant, David, to her chest with a shawl. Disheartened by poor crops in recent years, Elizabeth and Carl joined a curious crowd gathered at the *rathaus*, the town hall, to hear the agent speak. "Freedom from starvation and free land and jobs in America! All will be yours after a scant six weeks' crossing. Buy your tickets today for the land of promise."

Hands went up with questions for the agent who pressed German emigration brochures into upturned palms. Herr Schultz searched the crowd and found tired eyes that betrayed their owners' bone weariness from their struggles to stay alive. Two young men and a woman fastened pleading eyes on the gaunt shipping agent. Carl recognized the brothers and wife of the older one who lived in a crumbling hut next to the bridge the shipping agent had just crossed. Another family of earnest believers yearned for safety from religious oppression. In Prussia, most towns had a favored religion; this family practiced outside that faith and was likewise excluded from belonging to craftsmen guilds and social clubs. Others in the crowd lived in desperate circumstances; they had saved for years, scraping together enough marks to pay for passage to America, Canada or Australia. In contrast, the land owners, military officers and town leaders had few reasons to leave their relatively comfortable lives. In between were the targets of the shipping agent's appeal—those being pushed to leave by economic and political forces who could afford to do so right away. Carl and Elizabeth Tangemann felt pressure to leave their homeland by too little food, too few jobs and growing political unrest.

Carl accepted the brochure describing passage to America. That evening he and Elizabeth read each word, weighing the advantages and disadvantages of emigrating from their home in Sulingen to America. George and Wilhelm, Carl's younger brothers had emigrated last year, and they had offered to help Carl find work in New York. But, other family and friends remained in Sulingen. For now they had enough to eat and a secure place to live with Elizabeth's parents, but their own family was growing. They could not afford the larger home they would need in a few years. Famine and revolutionary unrest were their immediate threats.

Sulingen, Hannover, Prussia in May, 1847

A single horse's hooves laid heavy clops on the cobblestone street in front of the home of *Herr* Franz, mayor of the town of Sulingen. His daughter, Elizabeth Franz Tangemann, looked up from stirring a vegetable stew nearly ready for supper. In front of the home Carl and Elizabeth shared with her parents, sisters and brothers, a rider, erect in military bearing and uniform, approached hurriedly on a chestnut stallion, sleek with sweat. The rider dismounted and strode long steps toward the front door. Elizabeth turned quickly, and in a few hurried steps, called to her husband in the woodworking shop at the back of the house. "Carl," said Elizabeth in low tones, "a Prussian officer is here." Meanwhile, a strong knock summoned Elizabeth to answer the front door.

"*Guten abend.* My name is Captain Schmidt. Is this the home of Herr Carl Tangemann?" asked the tall stranger. "If so, is he home?"

"Ja, my husband is Carl Tangemann. I will call him," replied Elizabeth. She moved past her mother and younger sisters to the back of the house where Carl crafted a wooden cabinet for their kitchen.

Carl came around the corner of the house from the woodworking shop and admired the chestnut stallion at his front door. He wiped his hands of sawdust, and extended his hand, "Captain Schmidt, welcome to Sulingen." Carl smiled a greeting to his previous commanding officer from the Prussian standing army. Memories of army life flooded back. The camaraderie, grueling training and exhausting marches were legendary. Carl had coped well with the strict discipline of the Prussian *Landwehr*. He admired how Captain Schmidt led with clear orders and level-headed fairness. "Has it been more than two years since we last met?"

"Herr Tangemann, ja, it has been that long. How are you? How is your family?" returned Captain Schmidt. This was an unexpected visit, likely official business.

Carl replied, "My family is well. You met my wife, Elizabeth at the door. We now have a daughter, Dorothee, and an infant son, David, born in March. Would you like to come inside for a beer?" asked Carl warmly. "Supper will be ready soon."

"*Danke*, but I do not have time for a visit. I have come to ask you to rejoin the Landwehr as soon as possible. War has broken out with the Danes in Schleisweg-Holstein, and we need to build up the land forces for our Prussian king," replied Captain Schmidt. "I have come to ask you to join your old company as part of the officer corps."

Carl expected to receive this visitor and to hear his offer. "Thank you, I am grateful you have come to me with such a generous offer," replied Carl carefully. "Of course, I must discuss it with Elizabeth. You will hear from me by the end of this month."

"You are a natural leader of soldiers. I hope you will rejoin my company in the service of the King of Prussia. Your talents will be recognized and rewarded in the Landwehr. *Auf Wiedersehen*," Captain Schmidt bid farewell to Carl. In an instant he remounted the chestnut and clattered down the street, anxious to continue his recruitment mission.

"Auf Wiedersehen," Carl called in return to the figure disappearing on horseback.

The visit of Captain Schmidt forced Carl and Elizabeth to face their dilemma. If they stayed in Sulingen close to family and friends, Carl would be drawn into the impending war and risk death far from home. Or, they could emigrate to America and join Carl's brothers, George and Wilhelm, another risky path at best. If they survived the crossing, America held out the promise of opportunities for a better way of life. The young couple understood the stakes were high for their family and for their state of Hannover, Prussia. Rumors of war had invaded their homeland many months ago. Now that war had broken out with the Danes in Schleisweg-Holstein, it was time for Carl and Elizabeth to decide their future.

When Dorothee and David were both settled in bed for the night, Carl began, "War is being discussed in every *biergarten* in Prussia. In time, this war with the Danes may spread and threaten our peace and stability. Our home and village of Sulingen and our state of Hannover will need to be defended."

"If you join the Landwehr, you will be away for months or even years," said Elizabeth with emotion in her voice. "But, if you don't accept Captain Schmidt's invitation, what will happen?"

"Surely, I will be conscripted to the Landwehr by the end of the year," replied Carl. "But I may not receive the rank Captain Schmidt offers to me now. If all goes well and our side wins, I could gain favor as a battle commander, and perhaps acquire land in captured territories. Of course, we would need to move away from Sulingen in that case. If we lost, I would likely be wounded, or worse."

"Everyone is talking about war and revolution. Do you think rumors of unification might come to pass?" asked Elizabeth as she sat on the edge of their bed. "Could all of the towns and principalities come under one central authority?"

"That's not likely," replied Carl, rubbing his forehead. "Each warlord enjoys authority over his own territory. They won't give up their lands to a central authority without a fight." Although loyal to his king and fellow Prussian soldiers, Carl believed the army leadership could become subject to political forces far beyond of their control. "I am worried about staying in Sulingen for another reason. The Irish famine has spread closer to us."

Elizabeth was startled, "I know there have been food shortages on the continent. Cousin Sherzo brought word last month of food riots in Berlin. People plundered stores and markets to demonstrate against the high price of food. But, I haven't heard of famine elsewhere in Prussia," Elizabeth said, "Have you?"

"I did not want to tell you, Liza. In March, my local Sandstrom militia unit was on patrol when we found a family who had starved to death just beyond the river. They had recently moved here from the eastern lands into a vacant hut. We buried the bodies, but we didn't want to alarm the town. I only told your father. As mayor, he needs to know of these dangers," explained Carl with his arm around Elizabeth's shoulders.

"There is danger everywhere. All this talk of revolution. Prussia fights with Austria, and we are at war with the Danes! How can we ever be safe?" Elizabeth exclaimed, worry showing on her face. Carl tried to console Elizabeth, but he shared her frustration.

Carl and Elizabeth were trapped. If they stayed in Sulingen, they would be among thousands of Prussians living on the edge of having enough to eat. And Carl was sure to be plunged headlong into the upcoming revolutionary struggle for power in Prussia. Emigration was risky, too. The crossing would be fraught with danger from storms and shipwrecks. In a new land, they would need to learn a new language and find a way to make a living. They would encounter non-German speaking immigrants from other parts of Europe and other citizens of the United States. Great changes would come to their lives.

"If there was a way for us to stay here and build a life for the children, I would prefer that path. But, that is not possible in Prussia. It is time for us to leave Sulingen," said Carl, speaking in low tones what they had both been thinking. The decision was easier knowing Wilhelm and George were already in America. "The United States is not engaged in a self-defeating war. There, we will be able to put all of our efforts into building a future for the children, with Wilhelm and George, too." Carl looked into Elizabeth's eyes and saw assent. They breathed a deep sigh and embraced now that the decision to emigrate to America had been said out loud.

"Ja, it is time to leave Prussia. Let's leave as soon as possible," agreed Elizabeth with heaviness in her heart. "I have thought of emigration since your brothers left last year. So many others have left Sulingen and nearby towns since then."

"George and Wilhelm need to know of our decision to sail to New York," said Carl. "Tomorrow I will write a letter and have Otto post it when he goes to Hannover."

"And I will begin preparations immediately," said Elizabeth as her eyes caressed Dorothee and David. It was hard to believe they would become Americans.

Carl was eager to see his brothers in New York, but he dreaded leaving his parents and sisters. He felt especially close to his father. Friedrich taught him the saddlery and carpentry trades and they had worked together since he was a youth. On the practical side, Carl knew the saddlery shop could better support the family remaining in Sulingen after they left for America. He would miss his mother's jolly laughter as she worked, her strong, loving embraces, and, his favorites, *sauerkraut* and *liverwurst*.

Carl and Elizabeth set aside thoughts of the pain of parting to a later time, while they put their hands to work preparing for emigration. Elizabeth oversaw household matters. She and her sisters sewed clothing for the children. Shoes, blankets, trousers and a waistcoat for Carl and extra dresses and undergarments for herself were bartered or made by hand. For security Elizabeth painstakingly sewed their few gold coins individually into the hem of Carl's waist coat and her undergarments. On their journey, she would clip a few threads to release each coin individually when it was needed.

Carl read the shipping agent's brochure again for details about departure times and costs. He asked Herr Schultz about direct passage on ships from the nearby Prussian ports of Bremerhaven and Hamburg to America. He learned the least expensive passage to America was through England, departing from Liverpool bound for New York. Carl booked their tickets to depart on the *Talisman* from Bremerhaven to Hull, England, September 4, 1847.

FAREWELL LETTER FROM CARL TANGEMANN IN
SULINGEN, HANNOVER, PRUSSIA TO GEORGE AND
WILHELM TANGEMAN IN NEW YORK

May 10, 1847
New York, New York

Dear George and Wilhelm,

Greetings from your family in Sulingen. This letter is to tell you Elizabeth and I have decided to emigrate to America as soon as arrangements can be made. We will make the journey on the York-shire departing from Liverpool, England, in early September of this year. We hope to arrive in New York by the end of October.

Everyone is well except for David whose skin has an irritation. Dorothee is a fine, robust, happy child, always in some kind of mischief. Elizabeth has recovered her strength and will be ready for the ocean crossing.

As we prepare to depart from Sulingen, we embrace the hope of reuniting with both of you. Together, we will face the challenges along the way and find opportunities to prosper in America.

Your brother,
Carl
Sulingen, Hannover, Prussia

Finally, Carl asked Uncle Gottlob, a broad-shouldered, muscular woodworker, to craft a sturdy shipping trunk for their journey. He constructed a false bottom in the trunk for valuables, and on the lid he carved a "T," the only ornamental feature of this practical container. It would hold all of the tangible necessities from their lives in Sulingen. Uncle

Gottlob attached leather handles to each end of the trunk. In exchange, Carl gave his uncle the woodworking tools he could not take to America.

When it was time to pack the family's trunk for emigration, a swirl of memories hovered between Carl and Elizabeth. They thought of Sulingen, their childhood home where playmates had grown into friends. Most of their extended family lived nearby and came together for special occasions. They recalled their marriage celebration had been joyous for themselves, their families and the whole community.

"Do you remember this?" asked Elizabeth, wistful pleasure in her voice, as she packed a dress for Dorothee trimmed from her wedding veil. She packed four other dresses for Dorothee and six gowns for David, the same ones she had made for Dorothee as an infant.

Carl smiled and gave Elizabeth a warm embrace. "Ja, Liza, it was the finest day of my life," he said, recalling their wedding day. Then Carl placed two woodworking tools in the trunk, a planer and a file. He hoped to practice the woodworking trade in their new country.

Elizabeth tucked her sewing kit along the inside of the trunk. On top of extra clothing and medicines, she folded and gently laid the patchwork quilt made by her mother as a wedding present. Finally, Carl packed the family Bible on top of their other treasures.

LETTER FROM GEORGE TANGEMANN IN NEW YORK TO
CARL AND ELIZABETH TANGEMANN IN REPOSNSE TO CARL'S
LETTER ABOUT EMIGRATION TO AMERICA

July 5, 1847
Sulingen, Hannover, Prussia

Dear Carl and Elizabeth,
    Wilhelm and I rejoice to learn of your plans to emigrate. America is

a good place to live and find a better life. It is difficult, too. The English language is difficult to learn. We make a special effort to speak English away from the German-speaking areas of New York. Some people are patient, but other shopkeepers tell us to leave and not come back. That much I know of English. When we move west, there won't be so many who speak German, so we try to learn some English words every day.

Last week Wilhelm entered a marksman competition in the Kleindeutschland of New York. He made a good showing, but not as well as you could have done. Perhaps you will enter and win some cash prizes when you are here.

Wilhelm and I have saved most of what we earn working on the harbor. I am sending enough for you to buy passage for your family to New York. If you can do so, bring some money, too. We will help you with a place to stay and food, so you don't starve before you get a job. You are strong, so you will find a job right away. We are saving every penny we can to buy land out west.

God willing, we will be reunited in November. Every day we will check for the arrival of your ship, the Yorkshire. Together we will overcome every challenge in this new country.

Your brother,
George
New York, New York

Chapter 2
Waterloo Harbor

Emigration, the act of separation from home, family and homeland, began for Carl, Elizabeth, Dorothee and David Tangeman when they departed Sulingen, Hannover, Prussia on August 30, 1847. Carl and Herman Sherzo, Carl's cousin, carried the fully packed family trunk from the porch and loaded it onto the back of his delivery wagon. Carl's and Elizabeth's families, twelve in all, were gathered to bravely say goodbye. After a last embrace with their families, Carl helped Elizabeth into the back of the wagon, and then lifted the children into her arms. Elizabeth's head bowed to hide her tears. She busied herself settling the children on top of thick blankets in the bed of the wagon. Finally, Carl handed the carpetbag filled with food and clothing for the children to Elizabeth and climbed onto the seat next to Herman. He only vaguely imagined the finality of this parting from all he had known in his lifetime, but he felt his heart rip from its mooring as Herman loosened and snapped the reins over the four draft horses. The Tangemann and Franz family members waved through the morning mist, calling, "Auf Wiedersehen." In spite of his effort to be strong, tears came to Carl's eyes as he bid farewell to his family for the last time, the pain of separation close to intolerable.

The trip north to Bremen was slow and rough. For two foggy days the emigrants jostled over bumps and dips in a road still deeply rutted from recent rains. Carl and Elizabeth drank in familiar scenes from their homeland as familiar villages, streams and castles disappeared into mist.

The young Tangemann family joined the stream of emigrants flowing from across Northern Europe toward Bremen. Once they arrived in Bremen, they traveled on trains, river flatboats and in wagons, in the thousands forming a river of hope northward along the Weser River to the harbor of Bremerhaven on the North Sea.

Dorothee laughed when their steam train pulled out of the Bremen *bahnhof* bound for the town of Brake, partway between Bremen and Bremerhaven. They arrived at the Brake bahnhof late in the afternoon. Across the street Herr Weber welcomed the Tangemann family to Brake *Haus*, a small family owned hotel. After a supper of *sauerbraten*, thick dumplings and dark gravy prepared by Frau Weber, Elizabeth bathed and dressed the children and sang to them to as they drifted to sleep. The sun was well into the sky when the children awakened to the street clatter the following morning. Before nightfall of their second day in Brake, they received their last letter from Carl's father (*Chapter 1, August 28, 1847*). Friedrich had written and mailed it to them the previous week. Carl read the letter to Elizabeth and felt the seriousness of their decision to leave family and familiar surroundings. Yet he was relieved to know his father understood the necessity of leaving their home and homeland.

The Tangemanns boarded a river flatboat on their fourth day churning downstream toward the North Sea. In Bremerhaven, they met Captain Horst, captain for the *Talisman*, a German packet ship, destination Hull, England. Dorothee laughed when the ship moved onto the open ocean, especially when it tipped enough for her to fall and roll on the main deck. In the mild weather of late summer, crossing the North Sea was easy, and they arrived in Hull, September 5, 1847. Noticing many travelers were sick in Hull, Carl booked passage for the earliest available train to Liverpool.

Illness around them reinforced Elizabeth's sense of being in a strange land, already far from their familiar surroundings and language in Sulingen. They kept to themselves to avoid exposure to fevers and for mutual comfort. Early on Monday, September 6, their cross-country train departed for Liverpool. They arrived at 3:00 in the afternoon in that major harbor city on the west coast of England

In 1847, Liverpool, England was the busiest port for emigration from Europe to America. A flood of emigrants fled Europe seeking safety in distant lands. From Ireland alone, over one-fourth of the population had left to escape the famine of 1846 through 1847. Shipping agents, eager to accommodate this human tide of emigrants, conducted a brisk business selling steerage tickets from Liverpool to America. To serve the burgeoning emigrant trade, the population of Liverpool increased fourfold in the 1840s and 1850s, from 20,000 to 80,000 souls.

From the Liverpool train station, Elizabeth gestured to two ships just entering Waterloo Harbor. "Will our ship be like one of those?" One flew an American flag; the other was Swedish. They joined dozens of ships moving slowly to and from docking points along the pier.

"Herr Weber explained about ships arriving from America. They are filled with cotton to feed the textile mills in Manchester, England. By tomorrow, they will be unloaded, and family bunks will be quickly constructed for steerage class passengers like us crossing to America," shared Carl. "For the low price we paid, I don't mind sleeping where cotton bales rested on the trip from America." In Waterloo Harbor, Carl witnessed firsthand how cotton, shipping agents, packet ships and emigrants fit together like cogs in the textile machines making handsome profits for shipping companies, plantations and textile companies alike.

Having surveyed the harbor, Carl led his family to an inexpensive-looking hotel near the Liverpool Terminal at Crown Street. The droopy-eyed inn keeper charged double what Carl had paid in Hull for a night's lodging. Gulping, Carl paid the charge, relieved to have found a safe haven for his family until their departure for America.

Early the morning of September 10, rippling sails of the *Yorkshire* beckoned to Carl, Elizabeth, Dorothee and David Tangemann. Once outside their hotel, Carl caught the eye of a tall, brawny porter and nodded toward the pier where the *Yorkshire* waited. He hoisted the family trunk and balanced it loosely on a beefy shoulder. Bobbing like a cork, the tiny Tangemann entourage waded through the crowd flowing downward toward clipper ships, packet ships and a passenger steamer.

Elizabeth followed the porter while infant David slept lightly in the homespun shawl tied securely over his mother's shoulder. The shawl had been woven by Elizabeth's sister, Katharina, for the Atlantic crossing and life in America. Following closely, Carl carried wiggly Dorothee while watching protectively over his wife and porter. As the pulsating crowd thickened and jostled, Carl and Elizabeth wove through throngs of travelers, sweaty, panting and puffing for air. Carl practiced the English phrases he had learned, "pardon" and "thank you," to maneuver through the crowd. Nearer the *Yorkshire* he reverted to his native "*bitte*" in a louder pitch to push past the crush of appendages. Carl felt the press of bodies and knew this trip was a gamble of flesh and blood against the promise of safety and security in America.

The Tangemanns rounded a corner, and the River Mersey of Waterloo Harbor came into sight. Carl caught the movement of a sly hand in the corner of his eye. It slithered into the breast pocket of a fellow traveler in a smooth bump-and-take motion. Within reach of the thief, Carl extended his right arm reflexively and grabbed the wallet just as quickly yelling, "*Alto*, alto!" The victim felt his pocket for his missing wallet, and let out a roar of rage. Carl extended the wallet in his direction. Instantly, the thief dropped below elbows and sank cowardly out of sight. A policeman noticed the commotion, but could not find the sneaky pickpocket among the human flood.

"Thank you, thank you," exclaimed a surprised and grateful Irish emigrant. He had nearly lost his official papers of emigration, ticket for passage to America, and most of his cash. He secured the wallet in another inner pocket and buttoned it securely to prevent another theft. Emigration was his only escape from the Irish famine that had claimed thousands of lives in his home country. Today, his ticket on this one ship was his only chance to leave English shores alive.

The Customs House came quickly into view, and the Tangemanns' porter paused at the door to the medical examination room. With tickets for passage and emigration papers in hand, Carl shepherded his family through the medical examination. "Next," called the English doctor who gave but a few seconds of cursory attention to the Tangemanns. Not being obviously ill, their emigration papers were stamped "Medical Approval," and the line moved quickly through the Customs House and back out to the pier.

Carl spotted their porter back on the pier, head and shoulders above most of the crowd. The *Yorkshire* was within 20 yards when the Tangemanns' porter slowed his pace. They approached the sloping, slippery gang plank, taking in their sea-going home for the next several weeks.

The packet ship, a veteran of numerous crossings, was solidly built out of English oak and worn, yet sturdy brass fittings. High above deck, the main mast swayed gently. Seamen trimmed the sails to ready the ship for departure.

Over one hundred passengers boarded the *Yorkshire* ahead of Carl's family. The crowd parted for crew following orders to stow and secure cargo; the rhythm of final preparations seemed to soothe passengers and crew alike. Sailors climbed the main mast checking sails. Below, gaunt sailors grunted audibly as they hefted barrels of rice, wheat and oats onto their shoulders. With long strides they crossed the main deck, and passed their burdens to fellow crew members who delivered them below. Both human and material cargo shared the steerage quarters.

Carl looked up at the English flag worn with the dignity of repeated voyages and successful enterprise. Captain Smith was in command of his ninth return voyage to America and confident of another lucrative outcome. His optimism seemed in contrast to the heavy emotions of emigrants being played out on the main deck.

Carl supported her arm as Elizabeth climbed the oily gang-plank. Tears streamed down her face. She ached in body and soul, already missing her home, her family, her life as a daughter, a mother, a sister, a respected community member and a speaker of the German language. She knew few emigrants ever returned to their native land. And she was afraid, not for herself, but for her two small children embarking on a hazardous journey with an unknown outcome.

Once on board, Elizabeth stepped to the right, leaned against the worn oak bull rail and turned to drink in the Waterloo harbor. Through tears she saw haphazard tenements, boisterous English pubs, and the imposing Custom House. Far removed from familiar faces and places in Sulingen, she felt the finality of departure from England even more than when her eyes met those of her parents for the last time. Once the *Yorkshire* cleared Waterloo Harbor, she knew she would never see this harbor, Europe or her beloved home in Sulingen again.

"So many ships and all of these people. Where have they come from?" asked Elizabeth. Dozens of sailing ships, thousands of passengers, endless barrels and boxes of cargo along with crew and ships' captains crowded the sodden wood piers along the River Mersey and Waterloo Harbor.

"Many are Irish, starving and afraid to stay in the old country. Others like us are from the continent. I heard many people in Prussia have already left. There will be many German speak-ers in America," predicted Carl. Shipping companies saw the opportunity to fill ships bound for America with European emi-grants eager to flee and willing to risk their lives for tales of bounteous opportunities.

Carl relaxed and considered the heaps of squarish bundles stacked on the pier. "Do you see the bales of cotton, there on the pier?" Carl pointed. "Our innkeeper told me that packet ships, like our *Yorkshire*, bring cotton from America to the textile mills around Manchester. When they make the return voyage to America, they take emigrants like us to the new world along with finished English textiles," continued Carl.

"Those cheap English linens, cottons and woolens are putting weavers like my sisters out of business," exclaimed Elizabeth. "Our homespun can't measure up to machine woven goods at a cheaper price." When they thought of home, the gravity of emigration again swept over the young couple.

Carl put his arm around Elizabeth's shoulders and breathed a prayer of thanks for safe travel across the North Sea and the English countryside. Silently, he vowed in his heart to protect his family from the perils of their impending ocean journey. His face revealed both the pain of leaving and his determination to succeed in America.

Elizabeth's biggest worry on the ocean journey was David's health. At five months of age he had suckled well and gained weight. But he coughed often and cried loudly day and night. Elizabeth watched him closely and believed he coughed less and slept a little better compared to Dorothee at the same age. His navel had a rash that had only partly healed with the ointment from Carl's family. A fall crossing before winter set in was best for David's health. Still, she worried.

Dorothee, Carl's rosy, round-faced toddler, turned and looked over her father's shoulder, charmed by the bustle of workers and movement of bales, boxes and barrels. She babbled, "Dat...dat?" as she pointed to the sailors carrying barrels of salt pork and hardtack over the gang plank and down the wooden ladder to the hold. "That is a sailor...That is the sail...That is the rope," he explained. Dorothee asked, "Who dat?" as she pointed to a sailor looking behind every box and barrel as if he had lost something.

Captain Smith called out to three sailors to conduct the same search in other parts of the main deck, "Make sure there are no stowaways on board ship."

The taller sailor commented, "Without a bed, food or water, the poor devils won't survive. Better to find 'em and put 'em ashore." When the three sailors had conducted a thorough search, one called out, "Captain Smith, no stowaways found. The ship is ready to cast off."

Soon, giggling Dorothee wiggled and slipped out of her father's arms. She ran across the deck, straight for a coil of thick rope. Carl bounded after her, scooped her up in his arms making her giggle even more. "Down, down," she squealed.

"If I put you down, you must stay by me. Will you do that?" he responded. He waited until she nodded her head, brown curls bouncing, before he put her down on the deck. When she started to slip away, Carl bent down and grabbed her around the waist. She stayed on her father's hip until suppertime.

Carl knew their survival at sea depended on eating and drinking enough water and not succumbing to seasickness. On ship they were promised hardtack (a dense biscuit), sauerkraut, salt pork, dried fish, oats, rice, flour and cornmeal and sometimes hard cheese. Three quarts of water were allotted to each person each day on the journey. Perusing the provisions being wheeled on board, Carl mused to himself they appeared to be more plentiful than those supplied to his Prussian army unit.

Elizabeth heard an Irish jig drift up from below deck, compliments of a fiddle player and penny whistler. Irish passengers danced the jig with foot-stomping exhilaration, glad to embark on this adventure of a lifetime, full of relief from fear and famine. The sadness of parting from family and friends had been replaced by hope for reunion with dear ones who had made this journey before them. Soon others joined the lively dancing to relieve the tension between past and future.

Dorothee stayed next to her father's legs until Captain Smith walked by and gestured the Tangemann family to take their belongings to the steerage, below deck. "Welcome on board the *Yorkshire*. It is my sincere desire you will be well and comfortable in the crossing. Soon we will cast off for America."

"Danke," replied Carl. He understood some English words but was not yet able to put together more than a few words to speak his new language. On this English ship he hoped his family could learn to speak English before they arrived in New York harbor. Captain Smith turned to a deck hand and ordered, "Take this trunk to steerage for Mr. Tangemann." Carl understood "trunk" and "steerage" and followed the deck hand to their berth below deck.

The family bunk, outfitted with a straw mattress, was in a

corner of the open sleeping quarters below the main deck. Carl pointed to a space barely big enough for Uncle Gottlob's sturdy and beautiful family trunk. The most challenging part of the voyage, Carl mused, may be hearing dozens of people sleeping nearby, and using a chamber pot with minimal privacy at one end of the room. A curtain provided visual privacy, but sounds left little to the imagination. The smell of slop buckets would be with them throughout the voyage. Carl had experienced more primitive conditions in the army, but only in the company of other men. It was only a few weeks, certainly achievable with patience and perseverance. The rewards at the end of this journey across the Atlantic Ocean beckoned Carl and Elizabeth forward.

In America, the Tangemanns believed they would find safety far from the thunderbolts of war and the stealth of famine in Prussia. If fear for their survival drove them from Europe, hope for safety, freedom and opportunity drew them to America.

———⊰◦⊱———

On the day of departure, the undisturbed sea promised and hid all that lay ahead.

LAST LETTER FROM CARL TANGEMANN IN LIVERPOOL,
ENGLAND TO HIS PARENTS BEFORE SAILING TO AMERICA

September 9, 1847
Sulingen, Hannover, Prussia

Dear Papa and Mama,
Our journey to America has well begun. We arrived last week in Brake on the Weser River and received your letter from Herr Weber. Two days later we sailed from Bremerhaven to Hull, England, then by train to Liverpool. Tomorrow we depart from Liverpool for New York.
The weather was clear for crossing the North Sea from Bremerhaven to Hull, England. Many travelers were sick in Hull, but we

were not. We boarded the first train at Paragon Railway Station at 11:00 am and arrived in Liverpool by 3:00 pm. Elizabeth and the children are well and we are all anxious to be on our way to America. If winds are favorable, God willing, we will arrive in New York, in early November.

Thank you for the ointment for David. It provides healing of his navel and we trust he is well in a few days.

Please give Scherzo our thanks for driving us to Bremen, and I send fond greetings to Louise and Wilhelmina.

It is with a heavy and hopeful heart that we leave for America. Both of you will always be in our hearts and prayers as we remember our beloved families and home in Sulingen. Please share this letter with Elizabeth's family with our love.

Your son,
Carl (Heinrich Tangemann)*
Liverpool, England

*This letter and those following in this book are inspired by News from the Land of Freedom: German Immigrants Write Home.

Chapter 3
The Crossing

PREVIOUS LETTER (1846) FROM WHILHELM TANGEMAN IN
NEW YORK DESCRIBING CROSSING THE ATLANTIC OCEAN

July 10, 1846
Sulingen, Hannover, Prussia

Dear Papa and Mama,

George and I arrived in New York harbor yesterday. For forty-eight days our ship bobbed like a cork upon the Atlantic Ocean. Most of the passengers got sick at least once, especially when the ocean waves were as high as the ship itself. George was sick twice, but I was lucky. My worst problem was the boredom.

At first there was singing and dancing on the calm days. One musician, then another got sick with fever and vomited. People moaned all day and all night. I tried to stay on the main deck all that I could.

On the third week, a storm came upon us. The storm blew for three days and nights, howling and rocking the ship unmercifully. We thought the ship would surely capsize and all would be lost. On the second day of the storm, a Swedish woman gave birth in the middle of the storm. After that storm, it seemed we could survive anything.

The food on the ship was barely sufficient to keep us alive. I don't care if I never eat hardtack again. Even the sauerkraut lost its flavor amidst the smells of sickness and slop buckets. By the fifth week, I was numb from the motion of the ship and boredom with nothing to do. All of our stories had been told, and we just wanted to be on land. The saddest part of the trip was when two women who could not keep anything down starved to death.

We all worried about our fates until the New York shoreline came into view. Everyone cheered and thanked God who had brought us safely to America. I hope you and Elizabeth are well. How is wee Dorothee? Please give our greetings to Papa and Mama, and our dear sisters, Louise and Wilhelmina.

Your son, Wilhelm
New York, New York

On board the *Yorkshire*, sailors and seamen scurried along the gangway following orders and entertaining passengers on the main deck. From his perch twenty feet up the main mast, Joba, the captain's cabin boy, waved and shouted to all who glanced upward. "Hello, welcome to the *Yorkshire*." Dorothee looked up and waved back.

While Carl supervised Dorothee and bounced David on his knee, Elizabeth went below deck to explore their temporary home at sea. She found their family-sized bed in the corner near the ladder connecting the decks. Along each side of the steerage deck were nine similar accommodations. In between the two rows of family bunks was a table with benches on both sides. Elizabeth found their family's trunk and carpetbag with food and supplies at the foot of the bed. Then she stretched out on the canvas-covered straw mattress. Less comfortable than a featherbed at home, she hoped it would soften each night. The excitement of boarding, settling in and leaving the harbor had brought on a weariness that slipped her into a brief, deep sleep.

On deck Carl strained to understand the unfamiliar English being spoken around him. Other languages drifted across the deck, too: Norwegian, French, German and the thick brogue of the Irish speaking English or Gaelic, Carl couldn't tell which. Some passengers nodded and waved to other packet ships and newer steamships entering the harbor. They appeared relaxed as if on a holiday cruise across Waterloo Harbor.

Next to Carl a tall, whiskered man in a worsted waistcoat sat on a cargo box. The man glanced his way. "*Sprechen sie Deutsch?*" he asked. "My name is Herman Brandt. Are you German, too?"

"Ja, ja," Carl replied. "We are from Sulingen, near Hannover. My name is Carl Tangemann. This is my daughter, Dorothee, and my son, David," smiled Carl as he extended his hand in friendship.

"We are from Minden," Carl's new friend explained. "The crops have not been very good. The potatoes are rotting in the fields. The grain is too thin. We think it is better in America."

"We could all starve back home," Carl agreed. "In New York, my brothers have found work. They are saving to buy land in the west, and I want to do the same," he explained. It felt like home to speak his native tongue after hearing so many fellow travelers speak English and other languages in Liverpool.

"My wife and two daughters are on this voyage, too. They have gone below to settle in," said Herman. "Have you heard of Minden?"

"Ja, I believe Minden is south of Sulingen. My cousin, Martin Strauss, married a woman near there. Her name was Helga Schmidt," continued Carl. He smiled as he remembered many friends and family back home. Perhaps, facing the crossing with new friends would lighten the load for both families.

"There are several Schmidt families in the community. Some have farms with grain fields and cattle. I don't know them well," responded Herman, pleased to speak of familiar places and people in his native tongue.

The attentions of Carl and Herman were drawn to a family of four on the main deck. The husband was tall, of erect bearing, and dressed in a day coat, trousers and shiny black boots. On his arm, his wife rustled past, her blue satin dress trimmed in lace and velvet swishing with each stride. A jaunty navy satin hat with veil and blue parasol completed her outfit. The captain issued his formal greeting, "Welcome Mr. Swandike, Mrs. Swandike. We are honored to have your family on board the *Yorkshire*. Please follow me to your accommodations in our best first class cabin."

The Swandike family followed Captain Smith into the cabin, the long hallway running the length of the interior of the passenger quarters. That wide hallway served as the parlor and dining room for the cabin passengers. The cabin of the packet ship was carpeted and adorned with columns painted white with gilt trim. Near the aft end of the packet, the Swandikes were ushered into the largest passenger cabin. Mr. Swandike and their son returned to the main deck while Mrs. Swandike and their daughter settled into their cabin.

"The cabin passengers must have very different reasons to undertake this voyage," commented Carl. Herman nodded his understanding of the obvious class differences.

"Stand clear!" shouted the first mate. "Raise the gangplank!" Two beefy sailors pulled against thick ropes, being untied by their shore side counterparts, and the gangplank rose from its attachment to the peer supports. It slammed with a thud against the top deck, and the sailors secured it to the side of the ship blocking the gap in the sideboards. As if directed by an unseen hand, the bevy of sailors untied guide ropes and retied them to cleats on deck in preparation for casting off.

Carl, Elizabeth, baby David and his 25-month old sister, Dorothee Marie Sophie departed from Liverpool, England, on the packet sailing ship, *Yorkshire*, destination New York, on September 10, 1847.

———

The first night aboard the *Yorkshire*, Carl, Elizabeth, Dorothee and David slept much better than expected. David aroused for a feeding deep in the night, and the ship gently rocked him back to sleep. Most passengers in steerage settled down to sleep quickly. Even the snoring was gentle and rhythmic, lulling fellow passengers to sleep.

At daybreak Dorothee awoke first to the sounds of boots moving across the deck above. Light filtered through the hatch opening between steerage and top decks. "Papa, Papa…go up," she demanded. The family bunk that had been comfortable while asleep, became too crowded with the wiggly toddler. Carl sat up, ran his fingers through ruffled, wavy brown hair and pulled on his boots.

"Let's go up and see the new day," Carl agreed. All around them, families stirred and grunted their greetings for the day. On the other side of the steerage deck, Herman's younger daughter woke up fussy. Her mother hushed, "Now, now. We will go on deck soon. Breakfast is coming."

"I don't like the ship. It smells bad. I want to go home," Olga complained. Her mother, Marie Elena, smiled and hugged her daughter. Olga grimaced as they made their way to the slop bucket. After this necessity was behind them, the Brandts climbed the ladder out of steerage and breathed the salty sea air. With towel and soap in hand, they joined the single line to wash before breakfast.

Carl lifted Dorothee to the top rung of the seven and a half foot ladder. The rosy hue of sunrise dodged through transparent clouds, as she ran across the deck narrowly missing Joba on her way to climb on a thick coil of rope. The first mate shouted orders to the sailors scampering up the masts of the ship. One by one the sails unfurled, snapping to attention in the brisk morning breeze. As the ship picked up speed, the salty breeze cleared Carl's head of sleepiness.

Elizabeth emerged from below deck with David tucked in the shawl and a parcel of bread baked back home for the children. Carl offered to hold his son while Elizabeth and Dorothee joined the Brandts and other women in line for the washroom. She was thankful the ship had a few empty berths below. It meant extra space below and shorter lines for the washroom and meals.

While families waited in line, Captain Smith strode across the deck nodding to crew and smiling to passengers. If today was a sign, he predicted the journey to New York could take less than the average six weeks. Unlike his crossing last year that had challenged his skill to sail through three hurricane-strength storms, Captain Smith hoped for a peaceful crossing.

"Joba," Carl heard the captain call to his cabin boy, "Bring me my pipe." The grinning 10-year-old bounded out from the haphazard pile of cargo in the bow of the main deck and leaped up the steps to the captain's quarters. To Carl, he looked too young to be going to sea. To the orphan, Joba, the ship was his best home imaginable, under the protection of an honest, well-respected captain. He grinned and winked as he slid past Dorothee and Carl on his way to fetch the captain's pipe.

A favorite of the captain, Joba was also the pet of the crew. He made them laugh with tricks, and they teased him back. With pipe in one hand, he tried a single hand stand and received generous applause. Then he turned a cartwheel followed by a backflip. The passengers and crew cheered, "Bravo, bravo." After taking a bow, Joba leaped across the ropes and barrels to deliver the pipe to Captain Smith in the steering house. Smiles spread across the main deck as passengers relaxed from the strain of settling in to ship life.

Carl with David enjoyed Joba's antics. Carl took a deep breath to relax now that they had passed a restful night on board the *Yorkshire*. He enjoyed what the waking daylight revealed on the English side of the Irish Sea; solitary beaches and wind-driven vegetation bent back toward inland hamlets. In a friendly gesture, two fishermen waved as they dropped a net over the side of their tiny vessel just beyond a ragged, narrow cove.

The apprehensive passengers had heard tales written by friends and family about ocean crossings in grim, almost desperate terms. In contrast, the atmosphere on the *Yorkshire* was infused with hopeful anticipation, laced with music, dance and stories of homes as vivid as this day itself. Passengers found others from their countries of origin and began friendships that would last their lifetimes.

When the breakfast bell rang, Carl and David on his shoulder moved down the ladder with Elizabeth and Dorothee. They found places to sit along the table in the center of the steerage deck. Reverend Vogel led the blessing with confidence as he asked for God to bless the food and provide for a safe crossing.

Carl's new acquaintance, Herman Brandt, sat across the table with his wife, Marie Elena, and daughters, Helena, seven, and Olga, five years old. "Mama, I don't want to eat this. Why can't we have porridge like you make at home?" Elizabeth and Marie Elena exchanged looks of humor and understanding of Olga's protestations. Carl was glad to see the two families begin a friendship filled with laughter, stories of hardships back home and dreams of their new lives in America.

———

Contrary to Carl's worst fears, the first ten days of crossing seemed almost pleasant. Lofty winds carried their ship of dreams over the tips of beckoning waves. Quickly, shipboard life settled into a routine of sleeping, eating, washing, visiting, playing. They spent most of each day on deck feeling the sunshine and smelling the salty ocean breeze. The children on the ship made friends easily. They ran and giggled when the deck tilted and they rolled across the smooth deck. Carl thought the reports of sickness and death must be gross exaggerations.

The following week the waves became choppy, and the winds did not let up. Still, most passengers spent part of each day on deck until an occasional rain shower sent them below deck. They played games such as Euchre while others sang and told stories of the old country.

On the morning of the 16th day on board ship, storm clouds appeared on the southwest horizon. They built in volume and darkened the sky, obliterating the sun by supper time. At sunset, the sun's blood-orange rays slipped through cracks in the clouds painting distant clouds hues of purple and fuchsia. The wind increased, and the captain ordered the sails trimmed. Sailors clung to masts with monkey legs as the ship rolled and they secured the sails with ropes.

That night, only Dorothee slept. David woke to be comforted by his mother's milk numerous times. Carl willed himself to sleep, but his body did not comply as it had when his army unit slept on the frozen forest floor. The storm strengthened, and the wooden ship creaked through the night. The first of the passengers resisted, then succumbed to seasickness.

By morning, the tormenting storm had moved east of the bobbing ship. With relaxed wind gusts, the sails snapped as they unfurled. Carl and Elizabeth breathed a sigh of relief, again hopeful they would reach their destination. They assured themselves Captain Smith was familiar with these ocean currents, storm patterns, and every plank and peg of the ship, and he could guide them to safety. They hoped that only this relatively mild sea lay between them and New York.

Hardtack and tea for breakfast. The breakfast fare was becoming monotonous, but nourishing. This low quality staple of ocean voyages was barely edible.

On day 22, a dense, dark cloud settled over the ship. Wind speeds of 80 knots and more buffeted the floating, wooden shelter from all sides, seemingly all at once. The crew secured cargo in the lower deck and tied ropes around textile bundles wrapped in oilskin, to prevent their washing overboard. They secured themselves with ropes, too, whenever they ventured onto the main deck.

By the 23rd day, the sea was still churning 20- to 25-foot swells and winds blew incessantly. Everyone was ordered to lower decks for their own safety. The only food edible in these conditions was hardtack. Nausea and seasickness spread across all classes, many could not eat anything. They knew if they could just keep down sips of water, they would recover more quickly than if they became dehydrated.

On day 30, the storm ceased. Every passenger and many of the crew had succumbed to nausea or become seasick at least once. Many suffered from both hunger and nausea numerous times. By the time the passengers were allowed to return to the main deck, Carl knew all the harrowing stories of crossing the Atlantic had been true. One needed a strong reason to leave the old country and an even stronger reason to risk life and death to cross this treacherous ocean to a new world. Carl heard some travelers question whether they had made a mistake to cross the Atlantic Ocean.

At the end of the week, the captain reported that all 310 passengers and 48 crew members had survived the week of weather horror. He estimated about a hundred, mostly crew and cabin passengers, experienced mild symptoms and recovered within a few days. About one hundred sixty suffered temporary nausea and intermittent seasickness, but recovered within the following week. Those remaining were severely dehydrated and weakened to the point that they were in danger of death either later on the voyage or within a month of setting foot on land.

On the morning of the 31st day at sea, the captain called for all passengers and crew to gather on deck. "I have called you here to report the condition of our ship, passengers and crew and the progress of this voyage from Liverpool to America. First, by the grace of God, we have all survived. You are to be congratulated for your courage and fortitude in the face of the strongest, most ferocious storm at sea I have ever experienced. Unfortunately, due to the strength and length of time we remained in the grip of the storm, our ship has been blown off course. We will not see the harbor of New York, as we are too far south. We may be near the state of Georgia, drifting south and west toward Florida. The ship has been damaged, but it can be repaired. The best course at this time is to sail south around the Florida Keys, then west to New Orleans."

A murmur rose among the crowd as the impact of these words penetrated and changed everyone's expectations from arrival in New York to New Orleans. The storm had prolonged their trip to America, and their landing would be far from their original destinations.

Disappointment showed on the faces of passengers and crew alike. "No one will know where we are. Our families will think we are lost," exclaimed a middle-aged woman.

"How can we travel to New York without money for travel expenses?" asked a steerage class passenger.

A burly man with a family of six added, "It will be weeks to backtrack from New Orleans to New York by sea, even longer by riverboat."

"Please, please!" pleaded the captain. "The company who owns this ship sold you tickets to New York. In New Orleans, you will be given tickets to travel to New York by riverboat on the Mississippi River or packet ship by sea if you prefer. Stay calm. Arrangements will be made for your accommodations and riverboat passage as soon as we arrive in port. For now, let us thank God for delivering us from destruction at sea and trust Providence to guide us eventually to New York." At this point, Reverend Vogel spontaneously stepped forward and led passengers and crew in a prayer of thanks and supplication.

Carl caught Elizabeth's eye and smiled. Yes, they had weathered a storm. They were alive, and they knew what they must do to stay alive and healthy. Now they must concentrate on rehydration and recovery along with everyone else on board. Elizabeth was weary from dehydration, and so was Dorothee. Little David seemed to have come through with minimal loss of fluids or weight.

Carl helped organize able-bodied passengers to offer water to everyone in steerage on an hourly basis. With each day, more of their fellow passengers gained strength. The fresh air, water and food were a tonic to weary bodies and souls. In short order, the fiddle player was healthy enough to spin out a ballad and a jig. Then the penny whistler joined when he knew the tunes. Sometimes a reel, sometimes a ballad from the homeland. They sang of sadness in leaving, gladness in living.

Friendships deepened as the passengers survived the storm together. Everyone needed to belong to a community in this time of trial. The storm waters had baptized the emigrants from Europe into immigrants to America. They were transformed by near death into new persons, confident yet unsure of their ability to survive in America.

Elizabeth passed the time waiting for their ocean voyage to end by sharing memories of her life back in Sulingen with Marie Elena and other women from Prussia. "I was born the third child of the mayor of Sulingen. Two older sisters were constant companions in growing up. We took care of our younger sister and two younger brothers. And Mama was a jovial soul. Our home was filled with the laughter and the mischief of many children. Cousins and neighborhood children often found *apfelkuchen* and dried fruit ready in the sweets bin. We had plenty to eat and enough to share with others," she remembered.

While enjoying camaraderie onboard ship, Elizabeth remembered similar feelings of warmth she felt while sharing housework with her mother and sisters, cooking, cleaning and weaving.

"Ja, that was a fine family. And now you have a family of your own, a fine husband and two healthy children," returned Marie Elena. She admired how comfortable Carl and Elizabeth were in each other's company, warm and loving. Elizabeth explained they fell in love early, but waited to be married until Carl finished his term of service in the standing army in 1844. They were married in Sulingen *Kirche* (Church), Sulingen, Hannover, Prussia on Saturday, October 1, 1844.

"Our first home was with my parents," Elizabeth described. "At first, food was plentiful, sickness was scarce and Carl's work in the local Sandstrom militia was nearby."

"Ja, I remember our first years of married life. Herman was so handsome…And we lived with his family. I had a lot to learn in the home of my mother-in-law," Marie Elena recalled, laughing warmly.

Elizabeth enjoyed these memories of home as she recognized her way of living there would never be the same again. "Our happiest times were the births of our children. Dorothee Marie Sophie was born August 21, 1845 and David Heinrich, March 2, 1847 in our home." Maria Elena told stories of her family, too, entertaining the other women until clanging pots and pans announced supper would be ready soon.

On the morning of the 35th day, the packet ship *Yorkshire* sailed in sight of the coast of Florida. Passengers and crew alike cheered as the tiny lump of land on the horizon grew steadily larger. Low vegetation on sand dunes and a few grass huts eventually came into view. The scantily clad inhabitants of the coastal area waved to the passing ship.

The captain set a course around the tip of the Florida peninsula and to the west along a string of islands known as the Florida

Keys. Captain Smith veered south, clear of the islands known for shipwrecks. The Florida Keys prospered from wreckage frequently floating to shore. He steered clear of the islands, shoals and coral reefs until he saw the lighthouse on the Garden Key at the far end of the string. On the starboard side a sailor spotted dolphins leaping in arched formations. Dorothee clapped and waved as the dolphins cleared the waves, wiggled their tails and splashed in synchronized fashion. Another passenger noticed the pointed backs of hammerhead sharks swimming parallel to the ship. Perhaps the sea creatures were a good omen for an agreeable outcome, in spite of the severe storm that had blown them away from New York. With good weather, the captain announced they may arrive in New Orleans in 10 more days. This news buoyed the spirits of all on board.

With diligence, Carl and the other healthier passengers continued the water brigade to supply all passengers and crew hourly. Most passengers improved steadily. But a few didn't. Unfortunately, Elizabeth was one of them. David's survival depended upon Elizabeth regaining her health. Even Dorothee who had bubbled with toddler enthusiasm at the beginning of the voyage had become weary of the shipboard routine. The truth haunted passengers and crew alike. Not all seagoing emigrants arrived in the new world; sickness and shipwrecks exacted a heavy tax of seagoing souls claimed by the deep.

On the 40th day, Carl felt Elizabeth's head for fever. Perhaps, she had a slight fever, but he couldn't be sure. He called the surgeon to check and was told she should have more fluids, food and fresh air at least three times a day. There was nothing else to be done.

By day 41, Elizabeth announced that she felt better and wanted to stay on deck during the day. Carl was overjoyed. Surely, the sunshine and gentle sea breezes would bring Elizabeth back to health. They could survive for five more days. On shore they would eat and drink fresh food and water. He would find a clean hotel and nurse his family back to full health. Not eager to sail the ocean anytime soon, Carl and Elizabeth decided to secure passage for their family on a riverboat. The riverboat trip had to be much easier—no open seas, land in sight, and places to stop along the way to disembark and take on cargo or passengers.

Passengers marveled as their shipboard home of the past 45 days sailed into the sprawling Mississippi River adjacent to New Orleans. Captain Smith had sailed into the tropical New Orleans harbor once before. He remembered humidity and stifling heat in a May crossing. November could be nearly as uncomfortable. He wanted to see his passengers safely disembarked, inspected for medical problems and turned over to his company head-quarters for processing to hotels and riverboat travel as soon as possible. Then he would board the first ship available and return to England. He knew this voyage had been his closest brush with death at sea. He was ready to retire from a sea-going life.

Finally, on the afternoon of October 31, 1847, Carl, Eliza-beth, their children and shipboard companions entered a calm New Orleans Harbor. Packet ships, tug boats, flatboats and steamers large and small passed the *Yorkshire* in a hasty bid for piers. On their starboard side, a packet sailing ship rode low across the harbor, fully burdened with cotton bound for New England, or more likely, Liverpool. Carl wished them a safe crossing, less frightful than their own. The shapes and sounds of New Orleans beckoned them while ships' horns and flatboat bells rang out.

On the order of the New Orleans Harbor Master, Cap-tain Smith dropped anchor on the far side of the Mississippi River across from New Orleans Harbor. The *Yorkshire* was not expected, and an agent for the parent Black Ball Company, New York, needed time to make arrangements for hotels and river or ship passage to New York. For 18 extra hours, 358 weary, smelly passengers and crew waited in the New Orleans heat. Everyone was hot, sticky, smelly, hungry and thirsty. Their legs longed to walk on solid ground. Sweat formed, pooled and dried in every pore. About half the time it rained. Most stayed on deck and allowed their clothing to get damp rather than go below in the sweltering heat. On deck, even a slight puff of wind bathed the travelers in a luxurious balm. The hours were lifeless as if they were observers, not actually living through the ordeal.

Elizabeth said little as she attended to David and Dorothee. David was lethargic, flushed and languid in the heat. Dorothee draped herself over her mother's skirts and dozed intermittently with bouts of fitful fussiness. Surely, Elizabeth believed, she would feel better on shore. Buoyed by the anticipation of relief from their traumatic crossing, Elizabeth ignored her returning fever. Carl thought she was sweating from the heat along with everyone else on the standing ship. Instead, the heat within and the heat without conspired to demolish her will to overcome this last obstacle on their voyage to America.

Carl observed that New Orleans was the bustling crossroads for slaves, immigrants and goods arriving from the sea, land and the Mississippi River. On every side of the *Yorkshire*, sailing and steam vessels moved into the New Orleans harbor with human cargo; immigrants from England, Ireland, Germany, Scandinavia or slaves from Virginia or North Carolina. An expanding economy into the deep south needed more slaves to grow more cotton. Outbound ships carried cotton bound for textile factories in England and New England and other trade products.

Sailing ships, frigates, barges and riverboats of different sizes and countries of origin vied for passage to and from the harbor. Carl observed first hand why ships departing Liverpool sold cheap steerage tickets. Ships leaving New Orleans harbor carried full loads of cotton on the main deck and below in steerage. On the return to America, steerage was fitted with temporary quarters for emigrants. No wonder the spaces were often crowded and stifling with poor ventilation and scant sanitation. The profitable cargo, cotton, needed no such luxuries. Human cargo was secondary. Low ticket prices on the return crossing from Liverpool to America merely filled up space in steerage and maximized profits. Carl felt anger rising as he realized poor European immigrants paid dearly to risk their lives in steerage conditions as they magnified the profits for wealthy cotton growers and ships owners.

While the Tangemanns languished through their last few hours on board the *Yorkshire*, Carl wrote letters to George and Wilhelm and his parents explaining where they had landed and why. He knew they would be concerned that a shipwreck had taken their lives.

Finally, the sun set on the last night Carl, Elizabeth, David and Dorothee spent on their ocean-going home. Across the Mississippi River, a raucous nightlife serenaded New Orleans, the fourth largest city in the expanding United States.

LETTER FROM CARL TANGEMAN UPON ARRIVAL IN NEW ORLEANS
TO GEORGE AND WILHELM TANGEMAN IN NEW YORK

November 1, 1847
New York, New York

Dear George and Wilhelm,

Elizabeth, the children and I have survived the crossing. A terrible storm blew us off course, and today we arrived in New Orleans. Everyone is weary, but alive. God willing, we will recover with good water and food and rest. Then we will take a riverboat up the Mississippi and eventually arrive in New York. We will all be together again soon.

Your brother, Carl
New Orleans, Louisiana

Chapter 4
New Orleans

LETTER FROM CARL TANGEMAN UPON ARRIVAL IN NEW ORLEANS
TO HIS PARENTS IN SULINGEN, HANNOVER, PRUSSIA

November 1, 1847
Sulingen, Hannover, Prussia

Dear Papa and Mama,
It is with great surprise and gratitude I write to you from New Orleans. We arrived in the New Orleans harbor today. By tomorrow we will be on shore, if it pleases God.
The passage from Liverpool to America was difficult. For seven days a dangerous storm raged and we stayed below deck. The hurricane was so strong, our ship was blown far off course. When the sea returned to calm, we were off the coast of Florida, a great distance south of New York. The only course open was to sail around the Florida peninsula and on to the port of New Orleans.
Elizabeth and the children are quite weary. In the storm the ship rolled violently from side to side, and the food was poor. Everyone was sick, but we recovered once the storm was past. Now that we will be ashore tomorrow, I am confident good food, water and rest will bring

us back to full health. Please pray for us for good health. Soon we will journey to New York on a riverboat and join George and Wilhelm.

Your son,
Carl
New Orleans, Louisiana

On November 1, 1847, passengers and crew of the *Yorkshire* were exhausted and eager to set feet on solid ground. "Good morning passengers and crew!" announced Captain Smith, worry lines smoothing on his forehead. "Soon we will disembark at New Orleans harbor. A crew member will bring your trunks and luggage up on deck and over the gangplank. First, you will be divided into groups based on your country of origin. You will have a guide who can speak your language. Next, you will see the medical examiner. Finally, you will register with the immigration authority. From there your guide will have tickets and accompany you to the proper train that will take you to your hotel. Your hotel bill will be paid for three nights. In that time, we will secure passage for you on a riverboat traveling up the Mississippi River to St. Louis and east by train. Or you may continue east on the Ohio River to Cincinnati, Ohio. From thence via canal boat to New York. If you prefer a packet ship, you will be booked on a packet ship following the coast to New York, a four-week ocean journey." The murmur of the crowd revealed their aversion to either mode of travel, and their simultaneous eagerness to resume their journey from New Orleans to New York.

At the confluence of the Mississippi River and the Gulf of Mexico, New Orleans was a seaport as well as a river port. Carl and Herman discussed their observations that New Orleans connected the American heartland with the rest of the world. In every direction, ships and boats were being unloaded and loaded by the sweaty muscles of thousands of men. Pork from Cincinnati, grains and cotton arrived from the interior of the country, while livestock, seeds, implements and consumer goods were packed and loaded on to river steamers plying their way upstream. Traders in New Orleans markets became rich handling such trades.

The young Tangeman family made its way down the gangplank and was assigned to Ernst, along with 24 others from Germanic lands. He led them to the medical building for examination. The medical officer barely looked up at the Tangeman family members. He mistook signs of illness for the fatigue that plagued passengers disembarking from an ocean voyage. With medical papers properly stamped, they proceeded to the immigration office housed in the Customs House. Weary, but relieved, Carl and Elizabeth stayed close to the Brandt family. Both families had learned some English, but now that they were in New Orleans, Carl thought French might have been more practical. In cursory fashion, the French-speaking immigration authority agent wrote their names, ages, countries of origin and occupations on the daily log of immigrants entering the US through the port of New Orleans. Ernst helped each family complete the required paperwork.

As the last German family completed official entry into the United States, Ernst led his charges to a horse-drawn train leaving for the German Coast, an area on the Mississippi River about 20 miles upstream from New Orleans. The German Coast had been settled a few generations earlier by German immigrants who worked to maintain their German language and culture. Carl breathed a sigh of relief at this news of a German-speaking community. With trunks and baggage stowed on board, they set off for the Gruenwald Hotel in the heart of the German Coast.

The Tangemans settled into comfortable seats across from their friends, the Brandt family. Carl first noticed how excited the Brandt children were to take in the new sights along the tracks, but his children were too weary to notice their surroundings. He held Dorothee asleep on his shoulder. David hardly stirred when they boarded the train dozing on his mother's lap. Perhaps it was just as well, Carl thought. The time on the train would pass for them more quickly if they slept.

At the German Coast train station, Ernst led the travelers across the street to the three-story Gruenwald Hotel. He booked rooms for the six families, three single individuals and himself. With the help of a porter, he made sure all belongings were safely delivered to each room and bath water ordered to be delivered as soon as possible.

Carl helped his family settle into their hotel room up the broad stairway to a dimly lit, wood-paneled hallway. The room was furnished with a double bed along with a large crib for Dorothee, dresser and wash stand. David would sleep with his parents. First, Carl helped Elizabeth remove her trip-heavy clothing and take a bath. That was when he first noticed her fever and flushed upper chest with small reddish spots. She assured him she would feel better with food, water and sleep. Elizabeth pulled on her least soiled shift and dropped onto the bed, asleep in three seconds. Without thinking twice, Carl undressed Dorothee and bathed her, half asleep. He found her least dirty shift, dressed her and lay her in the crib. She had a slight fever, too. Finally, Carl bathed his son. Carl's broad hands held the infant securely on his back, then front. David woke up enough to gurgle his delight in the warm water. In a few moments David was asleep next to his mother. After his own bath, Carl gathered up all of their trip clothing and delivered it to the reception desk. He asked for laundry services and questioned when the clothing could be returned. "Tomorrow morning," the friendly clerk replied with a smile.

"Can you direct me to a nearby restaurant?" inquired Carl. The clerk gestured across the hallway to the hotel's dining room where Carl ordered sauerbraten with potato dumplings and began to feel at home in his new country. At last, Carl relaxed in the assurance he could provide food and shelter for his family. He expected they would recover much strength in their three days at Gruenwald Hotel. At the end of the meal, Carl asked for a plate of the same for Elizabeth and Dorothee to share, along with flasks of healthy, fresh water and beer.

The next four days were a blur as they unfolded and they remained so in Carl's memory in the years to come. On Tuesday morning, November 2, David woke up with a wail that split Elizabeth's head. Holding him with aching arms, she tried to nurse him, but he was restless and unsatisfied. Carl roused and gathered Dorothee close to his chest. She was warm with fever, and fussy, too. He reached for the flask of water and held it to her lips. She quieted down and drank several swallows.

"Dorothee, would you like to eat? Here is bread and butter," Carl offered. She stared at the food before she laid her head on Carl's shoulder.

"Mama, mama…," Dorothee pleaded, reaching for her mother, and he handed her over to Elizabeth.

In a few moments, Carl was dressed and moving toward the door. "I'm going to the reception desk. Our clothes should be clean by now. Will you be all right until I return?" Elizabeth nodded her head, and he slipped out of the hotel room door.

Carl greeted the morning clerk, *"Guten morgan."* After exchanging a few pleasantries in German, he picked up the fresh stack of clothing for his family, *"Danke."* She smiled and replied, *"Danke shöen."* Carl smiled as he thought about how pleased Elizabeth would be to wear thoroughly clean clothing for the first time since they left Sulingen.

At the top of the stairs, Carl heard Dorothee's screams. Hands shaking, he inserted the iron key to re-enter their hotel room. He dropped the clean clothing at the sight before him. Elizabeth was in bed nearly passed out with David beside her and Dorothee screaming on the floor. In three strides, he had his daughter in his arms. "Liza, Liza!" Carl pleaded. "Wake up, what's wrong?" He tried to communicate with Elizabeth, but she was feverish and in a state of delirium. Carl recognized the truth, his family needed help.

Clutching Dorothee, Carl quickly made his way back to the reception desk. He explained that his wife was very ill and needed a doctor. "I'll send for Dr. Stein immediately," the clerk responded. Carl rushed back to their room. Elizabeth's eyes were closed and her skin was pale, pasty and gray. He lifted her head and pressed the flask of water to her lips. "Here, drink this." She swallowed with great effort, and Carl laid her head gently on the pillow. "Liza, can you hear me? Open your eyes, bitte." She struggled to open her eyes and smile weakly at the only man who had ever captured her heart.

In a matter of minutes, a knock on the door brought Carl to his feet. "Please come in, Dr. Stein," Carl beaconed. "My name is Carl Tangeman, and this is my wife, Elizabeth, daughter, Dorothee and son, David. We arrived from Germany yesterday. I had hoped they would be better with food, water and rest. But this morning, they all had fevers and Elizabeth was nearly unconscious."

"When did your wife develop these symptoms? How many days ago?" asked the kindly, dark-eyed doctor.

"She has been poorly for several days. I thought it was the strain of the journey, the close quarters. She had a fever yesterday when I bathed her, but she could have had it a few days before. Everyone on the ship was miserably hot. I noticed the eruptions on her skin yesterday. She was very quiet, very tired," replied Carl.

Dr. Stein examined Elizabeth, especially the red spots on her chest and neck. After checking the children he continued, "Mr. Tangeman, your wife has smallpox and must be quarantined. I will send for a horse and carriage immediately to transport her to Charity Hospital. I am sorry to say, her condition is grave. As for the children, you need a nurse to help care for them. My assistant, Frau Helga Albreicht, will be here within the hour. I will give her instructions to give them fluids and keep them cool."

Carl struggled to keep a clear head. How could this be? How could she have smallpox? What should he do to help? He was stunned at how quickly Elizabeth's condition had changed over night for the worse.

The carriage and two attendants arrived within the hour to transport Elizabeth to hospital. Carl held her hand until they lifted the litter, carried her from the room, down the stairs and out to the carriage. When he was alone, Carl held his head in his hands, and tried to choke back the tears. Holding his children, clutching them to his chest, Carl couldn't keep the tears from pouring down his cheeks. Would Liza recover? Would he ever see her again? Life without her was unimaginable.

Frau Albreicht arrived within the hour. Her broad face was kindly and she brought a large basket of food, milk and water, clothing and amusements. "Guten morgan. I am Helga Albreicht. Please be assured that I have cared for many children and helped them recover." Remembering Dr. Stein's recommendation, Carl left his children in Frau Albreicht's expert care. He returned to the reception clerk and asked how to locate Charity Hospital. The clerk wrote down the addresses of Charity Hospital and Gruenwald Hotel and sent for a carriage.

The carriage ride to Charity Hospital seemed to take hours. Carl tried to take in the sights of the neighborhood of small businesses with the owner's apartments above. Although surrounded by fellow German speakers, he felt more alone than he had in his entire life.

Finally, the carriage driver arrived at an imposing hospital with four thick pillars supporting a portico over steps into the front foyer. As he stepped inside the hospital entrance, a kindly nun asked if she could help. "My wife... Dr. Stein..." were the only words Carl could reply. She gestured down the corridor to the right. At the far end, a door was closed with a red sign that read *Quarantine*. In a few minutes, Dr. Stein emerged from the room and gestured for Carl to sit down with him on straight-backed chairs at the end of the hall.

"We are doing everything we can for your wife. She is very ill. By tomorrow, we will know if she can fight off the smallpox fever. Until then, we give her fluids and keep her comfortable," Dr. Stein explained in German, his hand on Carl's shoulder. Carl had nothing to say; he was in shock at the gravity of Elizabeth's illness.

"You may stay here or return to your hotel to care for your children. For now, your wife must be in quarantine. No other visitors besides yourself will be allowed." Dr. Stein rose, shook hands firmly with Carl and returned to complete rounds with his other patients.

In a daze, Carl stumbled down the steps of the hospital and walked the 14 blocks back to Gruenwald Hotel. How could Elizabeth be so ill? After surviving the crossing, it felt unfair that she could succumb to smallpox in this foreign land. Somehow, he managed to avoid being run over by a milk delivery wagon, tall cans bouncing and clattering over uneven, cobbled streets. Once Carl arrived, he rushed up the stairway and fumbled for the key to their hotel room. Inside, he found Helga holding David while Dorothee slept in the bed where she had last been with her mother. Carl sat next to Helga and asked after the children. "These are beautiful babies," replied Helga. "But they are warm. Both of them have a fever. Please help cool them off with a wash cloth." Carl rose and walked to the scroll-design pitcher and basin, moistened a cloth and returned to the edge of the bed. He wiped Dorothee's forehead. Her glassy eyes fluttered open, and she started to whimper, "Mama, mama. . ." Carl pulled her close, feeling the warmth of her soft, chubby body. A knock at the door pulled his attention away from his daughter.

"Ja?" Carl responded.

"It is me, Marie Elena. I have come to see if I may help," she explained. From their room down the hallway, she had heard the commotion of Dr. Stein's attendants as they carried Elizabeth's litter quickly and carefully down the stairs in the morning.

"Please, come in," Carl gestured for her to enter. "Elizabeth has a terrible fever. Dr. Stein says she has smallpox. She was taken to Charity Hospital. I went there, but I only saw her briefly as she is in quarantine. Oh, excuse me, Helga. This is our friend from the ship, Frau Marie Elena Brandt. And this is Frau Albreicht, an assistant to Dr. Stein who has cared for the children today."

Marie Elena asked to hold baby David. When she did, his body was warm to the touch. "Has Dr. Stein seen the children?" she asked.

"Not since this morning," replied Carl. "We are about to take them to Dr. Stein's office at the hospital."

"Of course, that is best," affirmed Marie Elena. "Herman and I will keep your family in our prayers." She helped Helga gather the children's clothing for the carpetbag. Then she walked with Carl and Frau Albreicht down the stairs where Carl asked the clerk to call for a carriage.

The carriage ride to Charity Hospital seemed longer than the wagon ride from Sulingen to Bremen. When they arrived, Frau Albreicht led the way to Dr. Stein's office, David in her arms. "Dr. Stein, the children have a fever, too." As he examined the infant and toddler, he kept his eyes down until he had finished the examination. When the doctor looked up, his eyes were kindly, yet truthful.

"David's fever is rising, and his chances of survival are slipping. Dorothee is stronger, yet her fever puts her in danger, too. And both children have the red bumps of smallpox." Dr. Stein gave Helga directions to keep the children cool with damp cloths and to give them as much to drink as they would take, food if they were hungry. Seeing exhaustion on Carl's face, he ordered Carl to return to the hotel and try to sleep. "If you are needed, I will send someone for you immediately."

Carl hired a carriage and returned to Gruenwald Hotel. He fell into bed, weary as a stone.

Carl awoke at dawn on November 4, as stiff as if he had been sleeping on a bed of rocks. He washed up and went downstairs for a breakfast he barely touched. Quickly, Carl left a note for the Brandts with the hotel clerk. Then he walked quickly to the hospital in the most direct route. A walk in the early morning air awakened his senses as it forced him to remember the events of the previous day and the precarious state of his family's health.

Charity Hospital opened at 8:00 am. Carl arrived shortly thereafter. He retraced his steps to Elizabeth's hospital bed. She was asleep when he arrived, and she woke to his touch on her hand. Their eyes met before tears blurred their sight. Elizabeth knew her body was engaged in a mortal battle. "Carl, if I don't survive, you must find someone to nurse David.... And Dorothee is so spirited. She needs a clear and steady hand to guide her." Carl could not bear to tell his wife that both children were already in quarantine in the hospital, seriously ill with smallpox, too. Instead, he reached for the glass of water and put it to her lips. "Here, Liza, take this." She swallowed with effort, then turned her head and fell asleep. He kissed her hand gently and left her to find his children.

The kindly nun at the front desk recognized Carl and pointed to the left and upstairs. When he arrived, Dr. Stein was examining Dorothee. She tried to wiggle away from Dr. Stein when she saw her father. "Your children are strong and sturdy, and the fever is not as serious as your wife's. By this evening we will hope they have passed the crisis. They need as many fluids as possible. Perhaps you will help the nuns with this task?"

"Yes, of course," Carl replied. "Anything I can do to help, I will gladly do. Thank you for helping my family." He scooped Dorothee up in his arms and tickled her with his full beard.

For the next few hours, Carl gave Dorothee and David sips of water every 10 minutes, grateful for an assignment that could improve their chances of survival. By noon, Herman and Marie Elena Brandt arrived to visit Carl and inquire about his family. He explained that all three had been afflicted with a serious fever called smallpox. By evening Dr. Stein seemed hopeful the children would pass their crises. Elizabeth's future was less certain. Carl asked Marie Elena to stay with the children and help them drink water and cool their bodies with damp cloths. Meanwhile, Herman accompanied Carl across the hospital to Elizabeth's room. "The nuns are taking good care of my family. They are skilled and kind. Dr. Stein had arranged for everything they need." The grave look on Carl's face told Herman of his desperate prayers, his restless helplessness.

The two men arrived at Elizabeth's room, and Herman waited in the hallway, respecting the quarantine. In this unfamiliar city, Carl was doubly grateful to have Herman as his friend, someone with whom he could speak freely in his native tongue. The nuns spoke French much of the time, and effectively gestured their intentions to those who spoke other languages. Spanish, Portuguese, English and Creole (a mixture of French, English and Spanish common in outlying areas) were heard frequently in the hallways. Carl took comfort in this friend from the old country who had similar ways of thinking and who was sturdy as an oak tree to lean on.

Carl sat next to Elizabeth's bed and held her feverish hand. It was slender, smooth and sallow from the fever. He watched her sleep, breathing in shallow, raspy breaths.

—⊰⊱—

Throughout the day and nighttime, Carl moved between his afflicted wife and children, praying, hoping, loving each of them with all of his strength, all of his passion, all of his life. Carl stayed in Charity Hospital over 24 hours with only a few breaks for food or dozing lightly in a chair at Elizabeth's bedside.

Elizabeth, the steady center of Carl's life, died on the morning of November 5, 1847 in New Orleans, Louisiana. The children perished in the afternoon and evening of the day of their mother's death. Carl imagined them in heaven as they had been in life. David in her arms and Dorothee draped across her lap snuggled in the folds of her homespun skirt. This image lodged in his heart for the next 51 years.

—⊰⊱—

Herman waited at the hospital all day for the news of Elizabeth and the children. He was there when Carl collapsed in shock and exhaustion. Now he hired a carriage to deliver them both to Gruenwald Hotel. Herman helped Carl up the stairs, into his hotel room. For the next fifteen hours Carl slept. Meanwhile, Herman contacted the German Society of New Orleans for assistance provided to German immigrants. They sent Frau Frohman who spoke both German and English to the hotel. Herman explained Carl's situation. He accompanied Frau Frohman to the Stuben Funeral Home and made the necessary funeral and burial arrangements.

—⊰⊱—

On November 6, 1847, the funeral for Elizabeth, Dorothee and David Tangeman was held at a nearby cemetery in New Orleans. It was brief, attended by Carl, Herman, Marie Elena, their daughters, Dr. Stein, a nun from the hospital and the hotel clerk. A priest from the nearby St. John's Parish conducted the service. Words of comfort were eclipsed by pain and loss.

Carl had no thought of where to go or what to do. Herman helped with the details of paying bills and choosing a boat for passage. Herman would have paid the bills himself, but Carl insisted he had the money to do so. Even so, Herman's assistance was priceless. Years later, Carl's memory of this time was only a vague one of being led and supported to complete the unwelcome, yet necessary tasks.

Two days later, on November 8, 1847 the Brandt family left by passenger steamer for St. Louis where they planned to continue northeast toward New York by train. Carl left by cargo steamer instead for an opportunity to perform hard physical labor. Carl said, "Goodbye and thank you," to these kindhearted angels of sorrow, but the memory of doing so faded like the morning mists in the Louisiana swamps. Carl never again saw or heard from these true friends he felt God provided in his time of extreme sorrow.

On the morning of the same day, Carl boarded the cargo steamer, *Talisman*, headed north on the Mississippi River, too. He left choking grief to begin his recovery on board a working vessel. Physical work was an outlet for raw emotions that had nowhere else to go. He agreed to unload cotton bales, guide slaves in chains to new owners, and carry crates of chickens to restaurants, anything he was asked to do. Carl left New Orleans for New York, to find Wilhelm and George, because he had nowhere else to go. His brothers were all he had left from shattered dreams.

November 8, 1847
Sulingen, Hannover, Prussia

Dear Father and Mother Franz,
I am sorry to write that Elizabeth and the children died of a fever,
likely small pox, in New Orleans. We survived the crossing even though
a hurricane blew us off course from New York. By the time we landed,
sickness was all around us in the New Orleans heat. My hopes and
dreams died with them.

In deepest sorrow,
Carl
New Orleans, Louisiana

Chapter 5
Out of the Depths

LETTER FROM CARL TANGEMAN IN NATCHEZ, MISSISSIPPI
TO HIS PARENTS IN SULINGEN, HANNOVER, PRUSSIA

November 11, 1847
Sulingen, Hannover, Prussia

Dear Papa and Mama,
I am making my way across country from New Orleans, towards New York. The past few days have been the most difficult of my life. Elizabeth, Dorothee and little David departed this life all on the same day, November 5, 1847 in New Orleans. Now I must start again after all my hopes and dreams have been lost.
With accounts settled in New Orleans, I signed on a working cargo steamer bound for St. Louis. In exchange for my labor, my passage is free including passage for Uncle Gottlob's trunk. The hard work is helping me pass the time.
This country is not at all like Sulingen. There are people from many places, speaking many languages. In Baton Rouge, a town on the Mississippi River, they are building a castle that looks like the ones we know in Prussia. It will be their capitol building for the

State of Louisiana. It reminded me of Prussia and my family and friends in Sulingen.

I don't know what lies ahead. When I find Wilhelm and George in New York, we will make our plan together.

Your son,
Carl
Natchez, Mississippi

In November, 1847, New Orleans, the second busiest port in America became the crossroads of Carl's life between Elizabeth and his shattered future. As he had left his parents in Sulingen, he needed to leave Elizabeth and the children in New Orleans. But nothing in his life had prepared him to face this moment. Nothing in his future would compare in desperation. Never before had he felt completely alone. At this great distance he felt cut off from family and friends in Prussia, his precious Elizabeth, and at moments, even abandoned by God.

Carl relied on his military training to give structure to find a way through this despair. Goal—plan—action. What was his goal? Traveling upriver to find George and Wilhelm in New York.

What was his plan? Find the steamship *Talisman* on Pier 8. Transport the family trunk to the steamship. Board the *Talisman*. Say, goodbye from his heart....begin again.

What is Carl's first action? This journey had begun with this single step. For several minutes, Carl sat on his trunk, hat in hand, head bowed. A prayer, a promise, a plea.... Down pier, he saw the river steamer, *Talisman*, being loaded with cargo. Dark-skinned slaves and freemen alike hefted and carried barrels and boxes. English textiles, sugar and rice bound for settlers upstream. A young fellow led two horses across the gangplank to the far end of the main deck. Six Holstein cows and four crates of Brahma chickens rounded out the menagerie. Finally, Carl witnessed a press of passengers boarding with satchels and parcels, and he knew the time had come to leave New Orleans. Now he must act. Carl stood, hefted the half-empty trunk to his shoulder and moved slowly toward Pier 8.

Thoughts of leaving Liverpool came back to Carl. The excitement, the anticipation, the trepidation...all were missing from this voyage. Without his family this departure was flat, void of conviction. Alone, the trip was only barely tolerable. Carl was dependent on the kindness of strangers for life-sustaining human contact.

Mr. Butler, the steamer's engineer greeted each passenger. "Good Morning. Welcome aboard the *Talisman*. May I see your ticket?...Mr. Tangeman, you are a working passenger?"

"Ja, I am here to work. I will do anything," Carl replied dispassionately. He welcomed ten days of hard labor on this river trip to St. Louis. Beneath his sadness and the numbness of grief, he also felt visceral anger rising to consciousness. Muscles would channel his feelings into sweat.

"Stow your trunk, then report to Mr. Pardeau, the first mate, in the Frenchie hat," Mr. Butler gestured in the direction of a skinny Frenchman with mustache, striped shirt and black beret hat.

Carl did as he was told, anxious to get to work. Mr. Pardeau motioned to the pier, "Bring those boxes and jugs on board. Follow the big fellow." Carl was average height, but strong, especially in the shoulders. He lifted a bulky parcel, followed Kito, a dark-skinned slave who topped six feet, back onto the boat and deposited it carefully on the pile of cargo. In smooth, quick movements, Carl helped load the remaining parcels and water jugs onto the *Talisman*.

In short order, the cargo, passengers and stock were all secured on deck. Carl found himself crowded among men, women and children speaking French, English, German, Spanish or Creole.

Carl moved toward the group speaking German. At first he simply listened to his native tongue, bathed in the familiar sounds and words. Johann Entz noticed Carl's knowing smile when he described the food and sanitation on board their sailing vessel from Antwerp to New Orleans. "Guten morgan. My name is Johann Entz, from Oldenburg."

"Guten morgan, I am Carl Tangeman, from Sulingen, near Hannover."

"This is my wife, Anna, and eight of these children are ours," Johann replied, glancing fondly toward the twenty or more children playing a circle game. "We are moving to Missouri and hope to own a farm. Where are you going?"

Carl hesitated, "I'm going…to New York…to meet my brothers. Then we will see…." Anna noticed the sadness in Carl's eyes, and she did not ask more questions. As the *Talisman* pulled away from the harbor, Carl looked upstream, determined to take only the memories of his love and joy for the family he lost. With great effort, he thought of Wilhelm and George and wondered how they responded when the *Yorkshire* did not arrive in New York.

The *Talisman* joined hundreds of vessels moving up and down the Mississippi River, flatboats, keelboats, sidewheel steamboats of the gold-braid trade (uniformed officers in charge), tugboats and a few showboats. Demand for pork bellies, cotton and grains attracted heavy-laden flatboats downstream to New Orleans markets. Carl noticed dark-skinned, thickly muscled slaves in chains pushing poles to move the loaded keelboats.

Upstream from their steamer to the far left was a large vessel that resembled a barge with what looked like a long, tall, flat-roofed building. A small towboat was attached, pushing the towering showboat downstream. "What is that?" asked Carl of his new acquaintances as he nodded to the showboat. Johann tapped another German speaker on the shoulder, "Bitte?" and asked about the towering vessel with ornately carved deck trims.

Frederick Mulhausen, a veteran river traveler replied, "That there is a showboat. It docks along the Mississippi River, locals came onboard t' enjoy a show of plays, music and dance. This is the end of the season. From New Orleans, the cast will return to Pittsburgh by steamer while the showboat makes the slow trip back upstream. They will make the same journey next summer bringing entertainment to dozens of communities along the Ohio and Mississippi Rivers. Two years ago, I saw a show, and enjoyed it very much."

Near the stern where the cattle were tied, a shout spread over the crowded deck, "Stop, thief!" followed by a dull thud of fist striking flesh. The crowd turned toward the commotion and sent up a shriek. Mr. Murdock, owner of nine slaves on the boat had struck Elias Porter, a young man from Pennsylvania, on the jaw. Mr. Porter was sent skidding across the deck and down on one knee before he rose and charged Murdock, ramming him against the side rail of the *Talisman*. The two men traded blows to the face and chest while passengers gave them wide berth. Finally, a blow across the nose knocked Porter to the deck again, and he stayed there. "This here feller just stole my wallet. It must be on him. Help me look." By this time, Mr. Butler had arrived on deck. He pushed aside steerage passengers roughly on his way to the fight scene. He joined Murdock in searching Porter's pockets, trousers and jacket. No wallet was found.

"Bring some water for this fellow. Murdock, you better hope he's alive. Otherwise, you face a murder charge." A bucket of river water splashed across Porter's face causing him to shake his head spraying water in all directions. The water washed away the blood from his nose and face, but not the pain of a broken nose.

Porter blubbered, "Wh-wh-what happened? Ow-w, my nose. You dirty...." he exclaimed to Murdock. By this time Murdock had backed away from the scene of the fight, still smarting from his injuries and baffled by not finding his wallet on Porter. What he had not noticed was Porter's accomplice who had received the wallet when Porter pinched it. Instantly, he withdrew, removed over $100 in bills and sent the wallet overboard. No one was the wiser as all eyes were on the fight.

By nightfall, the crowd on the *Talisman* was calm, ready to sleep. There was hardly enough room for each person to lie down on the deck floor. Carl chose a spot near Johann Entz and his family. He slept lightly in order to help these new friends in case of more trouble.

On November 9, the sun rose through crackling fall leaves. Their first stop of the river trip was scheduled late in the day in Baton Rouge. Cargo was ready to be delivered when wood was taken on to power the steam boiler. Under the authority of

Captain Cramer and Mr. Butler, Mr. Pardeau directed Carl to offload cargo and replenish the wood supply for the steam boiler along with other cargo passengers and slaves.

In the meantime, Carl ate his breakfast of sausage and bread. For days his appetite had been flat. He knew he must eat to maintain his health and strength. Today he actually tasted the bratwurst sausages and German rye bread purchased in New Orleans.

Rounding a "*bight* of the bend" in the river at Plaquemine, the rising sun warmed the steamboat passengers and hit the crew square in the face. The captain squinted to guide his vessel to the left of the island ahead. He steered as close to the island shore as he could without hitting snags. The showboat, a three-story floating music hall, passed close enough to count the pigeons riding on the top rail. The showboat was quiet after a three-day stop in Baton Rouge. The exhausted singers, dancers and musicians were sleeping off the previous late night of rousing entertainment. The showboat had provided welcome diversion for an isolated city in a fury, constructing Louisiana's new state capitol building. Carpenters, stone masons and common laborers along with the plantation gentry and shopkeepers had packed the showboat twice each evening, six strenuous foot stomping performances.

As if in response to the riverboat, an Irish traveler pulled out a harmonica and began to play. The fancy jig led the children to hold hands and skip in a circle to the music. As the jig played faster, the children twirled and laughed, finally falling to the deck in a giggling heap.

In moments like these, Carl missed his Dorothee, her playful spirit. He pulled his leather hat close over his eyes to shade his tears more than his eyes from the sun. Slowly he made his way to the back of the steamboat and pretended to check on the animals. He affectionately patted the cows' rumps, then dipped a water bucket into the river. Along the shore on the right, cypress trees bent over the riverbank, draped with Spanish moss, a curtain for the hidden life in the bayous. Strange birds, wing-spans as wide as a man with broad, blue-tinged wings dived close to the river, mouths open to catch a fish. Songbirds serenaded the *Talisman* with cherry-sweet songs.

When Carl returned to the bow of the boat, Mr. Mulhausen was sharing tales of the bayous. Years before, pirates had camped in the bayous, hiding their pirate booty among the snakes and alligators. Most famous of all was Jean Lafitte, the hero of the Battle of New Orleans in 1814. He lived off pirate booty worth millions said to be still hidden in the swampy marshes. He was a fixture of life in New Orleans thirty years earlier, known to the gambling houses and to the city fathers.

Baton Rouge had come into sight on the right side of the river by mid-afternoon. As they approached the dock, the sounds of construction drifted down to them. "Secure the hawser," shouted Mr. Pardeau to the dock hand who caught the heavy rope used for mooring the steamer. Carl waited languidly near the cargo, ready to heft a box of textiles or a barrel of iron tools and carry them to the designated warehouse. Much to his surprise, as the noisy construction site came into view, it appeared to be a medieval castle. Carl never imagined he would see another castle like the ones he left in Germany. His army travels had taken him past castle ruins complete with moats, stone turrets and ammunition batteries. How could there be such a castle in America?

Mr. Burrows, a burly, bearded man of approximately 40 years of age, gave the order for the cargo passengers and slaves to gather at the stern. "Kito," called Mr. Murdock, the owner, to the leader of the slaves, "Call your boys to work." Carl asked Anna Entz to hold his waist coat while he worked. Carl joined the cargo brigade delivering boxes of sugar cane and barrels of rice down the gangplank, to the left and into the wooden warehouse. Within an hour, the cargo had been offloaded and the steamboat had taken on three additional passengers and enough firewood to power the vessel to Natchez, Mississippi.

Once released from work duty, Carl grabbed his carpetbag, the one Elizabeth had packed with food and clothing for the children, and ran from the *Talisman* in search of fresh food. With only minutes until castoff, he moved toward the castle structure. The center of the castle was a square, four-story structure complete with the crenulated rampart for defense. Around the exterior were six hexagonal turrets with the tall, narrow windows originally designed for archers to release arrows. Lacking time to fully take in this castle in America, Carl's eyes darted left and right until he spotted a woman selling fresh crayfish on French bread. He bought one sandwich for today and another loaf of bread for tomorrow, a chunk of hard cheese and a jug of beer. "What are those?" asked Carl when he noticed a bunch of bananas hanging from a long nail.

"Bananas, the sweetest fruit in the bayou," replied the woman. Carl held up two fingers, paid and quickly stuffed the fresh food into his carpetbag and loped back toward the *Talisman*. Rounding the corner he heard three sharp blasts of the steamboat whistle, the five-minute warning of departure. Carl crossed the street named after General Lafayette, hero of the American Revolution, and trotted for twenty yards to the dock and up the gangplank.

Carl found Johann and Anna and a place to lean against the railing, breathing hard from the exertion of moving cargo and a fast dash for food. His muscles relaxed from their workout and sprint to the center of town. "Johann, I found some fresh bread, crab, cheese, this fruit called bananas, and even some beer. We can eat well for a day." Johann smiled a broad thanks. "I saw the great castle, too. Do you know what it is doing here in America?" asked Carl.

"It looks strange in this place." Mr. Mulhausen explained, "The plantation owners have become rich and powerful growing sugar cane and cotton in this part of the state, but they have little population. They used their influence to move the capitol from New Orleans to Baton Rouge hoping for independence from the wealthy dons downstream. The castle you saw is their new capital building. It makes us feel at home, ja?" grinned Mr. Mulhausen.

"Ja, that it does. And, it gives me something to write home that no one expected to learn about," replied Carl, allowing himself to smile for the first time since he lost his family.

The cool night of November 10, 1847 brought morning mist to the river. The river travelers woke up, yawning to the sight of overhanging cypress trees and the sounds of songbirds waking up in Bayou Sara. At first, Johann thought they were in the midst of a swarm of logs, perhaps lost from a flatboat bound for New Orleans. "Carl, Carl! Come look at these logs in the river. I think they are alligators," Johann said with a mixture of fear and delight on his face. "Look at those teeth," he exclaimed.

"I've never seen anything like it," responded Carl. By then a crowd had gathered at the railing. Children squealed at the sight.

Mr. Mulhausen joined the conversation. "Alligators patrol all through these swamps. They are silent swimmers, always looking for a next meal. I hear tell they can sneak up on a feller fishing from the bank, snap his leg off and slip back in the bayou stream before he knows what happened. And if there's a child on that bank, that alligator can eat it whole before a squeak of protest. I've been up and down this river a dozen times, so I've seen quite a lot." At this explanation, the crowd moved back from the railing not wanting to test Mr. Mulhausen's estimate of danger from the bayou.

The presence of the alligators served as an alarm, focusing their attention on the draping tree branches. How could people live in this dangerous and mysterious environment?

Moving upstream, St. Francisville emerged from the shadows, a platform on the riverbank stacked with cotton bales and rice stores. From the river Carl noticed the General Store, a boarding house and drug store. East Feliciana Parish was followed by West Feliciana Parish, home of Bayou Sara. A horse-drawn coach line connected the two villages at the edge of the swamp.

"Alligators are just the beginning of swamp life. Pelicans, parrots, egrets and bugs galore. And snakes of all kinds," explained Mr. Mulhausen.

"Look, there's a turtle," shouted one of the Entz children, thoroughly captivated by the mysterious swamps along the longest river on the continent.

By Thursday, November 11, 1847 a drizzle shrouded the *Talisman* as it approached Natchez, Mississippi. Carl pulled his canvas trench coat tighter around his neck and shoulders. The rain brought his mind back to his days in the Prussian army.

Physical discomfort was a daily occurrence. He knew how to take his mind away from the present moment to a different time and place. That journey to his family in Germany was difficult, too. Elizabeth and the children were beyond imagining. He chose to direct his mind back to the *Talisman* moving slowly up the Mississippi River.

Natchez, Mississippi was a city set on a high bluff above the east bank of the Mississippi River. Carl noticed the ornate and beautifully built antebellum mansions that flanked the town along the river. The *Talisman* arrived at the port of Natchez-Under-the-Hill shortly before noon. From first sight, Natchez had the look of a regal city, even in the rain. It bustled with the activity of dozens of steamboats, keelboats and flatboats loading and unloading goods and slaves. Next to New Orleans, Natchez was the major trading city along the Mississippi River. Similar to New Orleans, it operated a slave market to supply labor for plantations hungry to produce record cotton crops.

Mr. Murdock oversaw his nine slaves unload about a third of the cargo in the hold. They quickly fell into a rhythm of lifting bundles out of the hold and carrying them to a waiting wagon for transport to warehouses and businesses. Unlike the other stops along the Mississippi, Kito appeared nervous, even agitated. His eyes darted back and forth, fearful and apprehensive he would be sold at the Forks of the Road market in Natchez.

When the last of the cargo had been transported off the steamer, Mr. Murdock ordered his charges to stand still. Kito frantically looked all around considering an escape route, but found none. With rifle balanced across his right shoulder, Mr. Murdock watched while his helper, Eli, reattached chains to hands and feet of the slaves. He instructed Eli to lead the coffle of prisoners up the road that curved through the town proper of Natchez. They walked a mile east to the town limits to the Forks of the Road Market for slaves, cattle and horses.

Unlike the slave auctions Carl had seen in New Orleans, slaves were advertised for sale in the local newspaper with details of age, gender and health. Sellers and buyers met and negotiated directly for the sale of slaves, a swift process that satisfied the burgeoning demand for slave labor to grow cotton.

For many years a few parts of South Carolina and near Natchez were the only areas fit to grow cotton in North America. In the early 1800s, plantation owners discovered a new variety of cotton from Mexico that could be grown throughout the South. The cotton and slave trade boomed to meet the voracious demand of textile mills in New England and England.

Kito and the other eight male slaves had been taken from their homes in Virginia to be sold at the slave market in Natchez. As soils had been depleted by tobacco in the seaboard states, growers looked west to the cheap land in the cotton states of Alabama and Mississippi. The dark-skinned travelers on the *Talisman* had been sold "down river" from Virginia via the Mississippi River to Natchez, Mississippi for resale. From there, they would be transported to their new plantation homes as chattel of new owners. Although it was no longer legal to bring slaves into the United States, the oversupply of slaves was transported from eastern to deep south states to produce abundant, cheap cotton.

In the time remaining before cast off, Carl needed to find fresh food and post letters to his brothers and parents. He quickly left the *Talisman* and looked left and right. He spotted what looked to be a shortcut under a dark overhang. Carl moved along the shadowy path that curved to the right leading upward. Two gaunt figures stepped in front of him, preventing his progress.

"Stand aside," Carl ordered. "I don't want trouble." The shorter figure crouched and poised to land a punch. In a flash Carl sent a glancing blow to his left cheek. The taller fellow struck a blow on Carl's shoulder that sent pain across his upper back. By that time, the shorter one landed his punch in Carl's face, drawing blood from his prominent nose. Carl spun to the left and kicked his taller opponent in the stomach followed by a powerful jab to the short guy's jaw. All three men were punished in the brawl, but the two thugs backed off to nurse their wounds. Carl withdrew up the winding path into the sunlight. He limped and ran up the hill to the commercial district, the shops, hotels and opera house district. At the National Hotel, he took the front steps two at a time, and through the double doors. At the registration desk, Carl breathed hard to catch his breath as he asked, "Can you please mail these two letters? One is to New York and the other is to Europe." He was anxious for his parents and George and Wilhelm to know he was alive in America.

The clerk replied, "Yes, of course. Sir, are you all right?" Crimson blood dripped on the registration counter.

"Ja, I am fine. I must post these letters," replied Carl.

"They will go out tomorrow to New Orleans. Within a month they will leave by ship for New York and Europe," and the clerk collected a coin for the service.

Carl uttered, "Danke, danke," as he turned to leave the hotel lobby. Outside, he stopped at a bakery for fresh bread and a sausage roll. In minutes he was back on board the *Talisman* with fresh provisions. His nose and back throbbed for the rest of the day.

LETTER FROM CARL TANGEMAN IN NATCHEZ, MISSISSIPPI
TO GEORGE AND WILHELM TANGEMAN IN NEW YORK

November 11, 1847
New York, New York

Dear George and Wilhelm,

If you receive this letter, you will know I am making my way across country from New Orleans, towards New York. Elizabeth and the children have perished to a fever in New Orleans. Now I am traveling alone on the Mississippi River north toward St. Louis. It is a long slow trip. As a cargo passenger, I am working loading and unloading cargo in exchange for passage upriver.

As I wrote from New Orleans, our ship was blown off course by a terrible storm in the Atlantic Ocean. Now I am learning more English and seeing another part of America. There are many Africans here working as slaves on plantations that grow cotton. Everything is different from our life in Sulingen.

Please wait for me to join you in New York. Then we will start again and make a plan to buy some land.

Your brother,
Carl
Natchez, Mississippi

Chapter 6
Northward

LETTER FROM WILHELM TANGEMAN IN NEW YORK
TO HIS PARENTS IN SULINGEN, HANNOVER, PRUSSIA

November 20, 1847
Sulingen, Hannover, Prussia

Dear Papa and Mama,
We are well in New York and we wish good health for you both, Lou-ise and Wilhelmina and the friends we have left behind. We think of you often and raise a stein of beer to toast your memory. I miss Mama's sauerkraut very much.

George and I have good jobs on the harbor. We load and unload ships every day. Now we are very strong, so that farm work will be easy to do. If we stay healthy, we will have enough saved to move west soon. Each day we check to see if the Yorkshire has arrived from Liverpool. We hope and pray they have a safe crossing. When Carl arrives, we will plan our adventure west together.

Your son,
Wilhelm
New York, New York

On November 12, 1847 the *Talisman* river steamer approached Vicksburg, Mississippi past rolling hills undulating to the crescent bluff, the throne upon which rested Vicksburg. A few miles from the harbor, Carl noticed shreds of what looked like cloth draped over low branches on the cottonwood trees and smooth clearings among the clusters of cottonwood trees. He nudged Mr. Mulhausen with a quizzical look. "That there looks like an abandoned Choctaw Indian village. It looks like they left some old buckskin hanging from the low branches. Years ago they lived up and down the Mississippi. About 15 years ago the government moved most of them to Indian Territory, over there, west of the river. The ones who stayed, mostly keep to themselves," explained Mr. Mulhausen.

"Is it true what I've heard that frontier Indians make war on the settlers?" asked Carl in German. "I've been a soldier, but it can't be like fighting for the Prussian king," he added.

"Some Indians are hospitable, others are warring types," Mr. Mulhausen explained. "If you go west, it's best to stay in groups, help each other out. Don't start trouble, but be ready if it... Hey!" he shouted. A sailing keelboat narrowly missed the starboard side of the *Talisman* on approach to the Vicksburg pier. At the last moment two muscled deck hands heaved forward and threw their full weight into poles stuck in the Mississippi mud. Applying all of their weight to the task, the boatmen forced the keelboat to pivot on the poles and swish clear of the steamboat, the *Talisman*. The passengers, crew, and, especially Captain Cramer sighed in relief for the averted disaster.

Mr. Mulhausen continued his narration pointing to river sites, "On the bluff above the harbor, you can see a few weathered walnut trees that have clung to the grassy edge of the hillside. Remnants of the time of Spanish claim to the Mississippi River basin. They called the hillside Fort Nogales, Spanish for walnut trees. Beneath the bluff, the three local women with long, black hair and dressed in buckskin are looking for wood to gather and sell to steamers like ours at the port of Vicksburg." Carl and the other passengers watched as the women paddled a flat-bottomed boat in and out among the willows and rushes along the riverbank, stopping to drag driftwood into their boat.

The *Talisman* docked amidst a cluster of keelboats bound for New Orleans. One boat was stacked high with barrels of pork bellies in the bow. Another held cotton, another corn from the fall crop.

Vicksburg was similar to Natchez, a port city close to cotton plantations on the Mississippi River. It was also the railhead to interior towns via the Vicksburg-Meridian Railroad. And harbors of both cities were stacked high with cotton bales ready for shipment south to New Orleans and beyond. Without a bustling slave market, Vicksburg seemed like a quiet country town. Stately mansions flanked the city, but it lacked the trading atmosphere and wealth of a slave market city. Lacking wealth, Vicksburg also lacked music, art and a life of culture that money could buy.

The dock in Vicksburg was wide and light splashed in the mid-day sun. As soon as Mr. Pardeau cleared the bill of landing with the shipping clerk, he gave the signal to begin the transfer of goods. Carl eagerly fell into step with the other cargo crew. Mr. Pardeau pointed for the men to begin offloading the rice and sugar sacks. Upon returning, each of the men brought back the cotton bales first, and then wood for the steamer's boiler. Carl fell into step, hefting the bags and bales, missing Kito and the other slaves whose labor previously cut the task in half. Sweat ran down the faces of the laborers. To Carl it cleansed him from inside out. He lifted each load of goods, and at the same time, began to shed the burdens of his heart.

Sunday arrived wrapped in wintry mist. At first light, visibility was only about ten feet beyond the bow. Just past Napoleon, a port on the west side of the Mississippi, Carl noticed cargo boxes and barrels floating downstream, bouncing off their outer hull. A voice drifted out of the morning mist on that Sunday morning of November 14, 1847, "Yo, out there....Is anybody there?"

Captain Cramer shouted, "Over here, steamer on the east." He motioned a deck hand to swing his lantern to draw the attention of the stranger, across the murky mist.

"Yo, Cap'n. Wreck up ahead on the east," shouted a nearly invisible crew member manning the pole on a passing flatboat. "Stay t' west bank," he grunted. As the *Talisman* cleared a slight bend in the river, the wreckage of a keelboat on upturned tree roots came into dim sight. Captain Cramer steered the steamer toward the west bank, slowing to maneuver among down floating flatboats near the west bank and steamers moving upriver closer to the center channel. Soon they were safely clear of the twisted tree roots and splintered wreckage, grateful for the warning from a sister vessel. Gradually, the sun burned off the rising mist, and the sun warmed the humid air hovering above the Mississippi River.

Beyond Napoleon, the river became smooth. With each passing mile, the *Talisman* moved away from the narrow, congested river where river traffic was coming and going to New Orleans. As maneuvering the steamer became easier, Captain Cramer cranked up the speed. The vessel labored toward Victoria, a port town on the east side of the river.

Among the English passengers of the *Talisman* was a Methodist minister, Reverend Olmsby, and his family. After breakfast, this being Sunday morning, he stood on a heavy, shallow cargo box and called others to join an informal worship service. He preached about Moses' journey out of Egypt to the Promised Land. That trip long ago had many challenges, similar to their own arduous riverboat journey. Carl found unexpected comfort in this message from an unfamiliar religious sect in a foreign tongue in an untamed land. At the end of the service, he hummed along as the Methodists sang forth a familiar hymn, "Rock of Ages," *a cappella*.

For the next two days, rain fell off and on, day and night. The travelers huddled under canvas shelters or squeezed together below deck to stay out of the rain and to stay as warm as possible. Stories were told of the old country, and songs were sung to pass the time. On the second day of rain, Carl took a turn and recounted the story of *The Mother Goat and Seven Kids*.

There was once upon a time an old goat who had seven little kids, and loved them with all the love of a mother for her children. One day she wanted to go into the forest and fetch some food. So she called all seven to her and said, "Dear children, I have to go into the forest. Be on your guard against the wolf. If he comes in, he will devour you all - skin, hair, and everything. The wretch often disguises himself, but you will know him at once by his rough voice and his black feet." The kids said, "Dear Mother, we will take good care of ourselves. You may go away without any worry." Then the old one bleated, and went on her way with an easy mind.

It was not long before someone knocked at the house-door and called, "Open the door, dear children. Your mother is here, and has brought something back with her for each of you." But the little kids knew that it was the wolf, by the rough voice. "We will not open the door," cried they. "You are not our mother. She has a soft, pleasant voice, but your voice is rough. You are the wolf." Then the wolf went away to a shopkeeper and bought himself a great lump of chalk, ate this and made his voice soft with it. The he came back, knocked at the door of the house, and called, open the door, "Dear children, your mother is here and has brought something back with her for each of you." But the wolf had laid his black paws against the window, and the children saw them and cried, "We will not open the door. Our mother has not black feet like you. You are the wolf." Then the wolf ran to a baker and said, "I have hurt my feet. Rub some dough over them for me." And when the baker had rubbed his feet over with some dough, then he ran to the miller and said, "Strew some white meal over my feet for me." The miller thought to himself, "The wolf wants to deceive someone," and he refused, but the wolf said, "If you will not do it, I will devour you." Then the miller was afraid, and made the wolf's paws white for him. Truly, this is the way of mankind.

So now the wretch wolf went for the third time to the house-door, knocked at it and said, "Open the door for me, children. Your dear little mother has come home, and has brought every one of you something back from the forest with her." The little kids cried, first show us your paws that we may know if you are our dear little mother. Then he put his paws in through the window, and when the kids saw that they were white, they believed that all he said was true, and opened the door. But who should come in but the wolf. They were terrified and wanted to hide themselves. One sprang under the table, the second into the bed, the third into the stove, the fourth into the kitchen, the fifth into the cupboard, the sixth under the washing-bowl, and the seventh into the clock-case. But the wolf found them all, and used no great ceremony. One after the other he swallowed them down his throat. The youngest, who was in the clock-case, was the only one he did not find. When the wolf had satisfied his appetite, he took himself off, laid himself down under a tree in the green meadow outside, and began to sleep. Soon afterwards the old goat came home again from the forest. Ah. What a sight she saw there. The house-door stood wide open. The table, chairs, and benches were thrown down, the washing-bowl lay broken to pieces, and the quilts and pillows were pulled off the bed. She sought her children, but they were nowhere to be found. She called them one after another by name, but no one answered. At last, when she came to the youngest, a soft voice cried, "Dear Mother, I am in the clock-case." She took the kid out, and it told her that the wolf had come and had eaten all the others. Then you may imagine how she wept over her poor children.

At length in her grief she went out, and the youngest kid ran with her. When they came to the meadow, there lay the wolf by the tree and snored so loud that the branches shook. She looked at him on every side and saw that something was moving and struggling in his gorged belly. "Ah, heavens," she said, "Is it possible that my poor children whom he has swallowed down for his supper, can be still alive?" Then the kid had to run home and fetch scissors, and a needle and thread and the goat cut open the monster's stomach, and hardly had she make one cut, than one little kid thrust its head out, and when she cut farther, all six sprang out one after another, and were all still alive, and had suffered no injury whatever, for in his greediness the monster had swallowed them down whole. What rejoicing there was. They embraced their dear mother, and jumped like a sailor at his wedding. The mother, however, said, "Now go and look for some big stones, and we will fill the wicked beast's stomach with them while he is still asleep. Then the seven kids dragged the stones thither with all speed, and put as many of them into his stomach as they could get in, and the mother sewed him up again in the greatest haste, so that he was not aware of anything and never once stirred.

When the wolf at length had had his fill of sleep, he got on his legs, and as the stones in his stomach made him very thirsty, he wanted to *go to a well to drink. But when he began to walk and move about, the stones in his stomach knocked against each other and rattled. Then cried he, "What rumbles and tumbles against my poor bones. I thought 'twas six kids, but it feels like big stones." And when he got to the well and stooped over the water to drink, the heavy stones made him fall in, and he had to drown miserably. When the seven kids saw that, they came running to the spot and cried aloud, "The wolf is dead. The wolf is dead," and danced for joy round about the well with their mother.**

*A fairy tale by the Brothers Grimm, adapted from Folk and Fairy Tales.

Looking around the crowd of children and adults spellbound by his recounting of the story, Carl saw smiles. They clapped to show their appreciation for this tale of care and devotion, a welcome diversion from boredom and the chilly, humidity of steady rainfall.

Dry, edible food was scarce on these rainy days. It brought out the best and worst among strangers. Carl suggested they stretch out the time between meals and all eat at the same time to avoid jealousy at seeing others eat. Water was plentiful; everything else was soggy. The steamer passengers imagined the fresh provisions they could buy at the next docking in Memphis, Tennessee.

The morning of November 16 dawned clear and dry. By mid-morning Memphis could be seen on the eastern shore. The spirits of the *Talisman* passengers soared. In the morning sun, the Gayoso House Hotel shone like a gold crown overlooking the port and river from the bluff above. Mr. Malhausen pointed, "You are looking at the finest hotel in all of the western states. In 1845, I had the privilege of staying at the new Gayoso House Hotel for three days. I took a bath in a marble tub with silver faucets. I just wish I could stay there today…(chuckles from the crowd). And they even have indoor flush toilets. Mighty fancy."

"Where did they get the money for a fancy hotel?" called out a man in the crowd.

Mr. Mulhausen continued, "Why, cotton, of course. Just like Natchez, Memphis is a cotton market, and slave market, too. If you trade cotton or slaves, you can be a millionaire in Memphis."

"Where did you get enough money to stay at the Gayoso House Hotel?" jibed another passenger.

Captain Cramer broke into the conversation, "Ah, that is a story for a cold winter night. Today we have sunshine and the queen city of the Mississippi River, Memphis, Tennessee coming into sight. Let's spend three hours exploring and enjoying ourselves. God willing, the bad weather is behind us. When you hear three long honks and one short one on the steam horn, you will have twenty minutes to return to the steamer. I hope you enjoy your time in Memphis!"

For the next half-hour the passengers forgot about the rain of the past two days. They talked about Memphis, what a fine city it must be with hotels, bakeries, haberdashery and fine clothing shops. From the *Talisman*, they could see hundreds of people disembarking from steamers and boarding trains at the railway station across the street. It was apparent to all, Memphis had become a crossroads between north-south river transport and railroad traffic moving east.

The *Talisman* was smoothly brought to dock in Memphis, with a little wait and a gentle float to contact. The Entz family and most of the other passengers welcomed this opportunity to disembark and feel the solid streets under their feet. Smiles abounded as they stretched their legs, walked around freely, explored the new city of Memphis and purchased some fresh food. Meanwhile, Carl joined the cargo crew offloading cargo and transferring wood and bags of flour, cornmeal, butter, pork and additional provisions down into the hold of the steamer.

A short three hours later, the sound of the three long blasts of the steamer horn caught Mr. Entz' attention. He turned to Mrs. Entz, "Mother, it's time to finish and return to the *Talisman*." They laughed and shared their off boat adventures in Memphis. "Fresh bread and cheese," exclaimed the oldest Entz daughter to her mother. "And did you see the fine dresses the ladies wore? The lace was from Paris!"

"I did not expect to find a refined city so far inland," responded Mrs. Entz.

"Did you see the construction of so many new buildings in Memphis? A lot of people are coming for jobs. I heard German and many other languages. They are building Memphis with the labor of immigrants," commented Mr. Entz. "If we cannot make a living on the farm in Missouri, I could find work right here in Memphis." Mrs. Entz nodded and smiled her agreement. They were happy at the thought of another opportunity for employment in their new country.

"Come, girls. Find your places on the boat," directed Anna Entz. "It is only a few more days to St. Louis. Surely, the worst of the journey is behind us." With fresh provisions and a sunny day, the Entz family, along with other passengers and crew of the *Talisman* were in the best of spirits. Each day on the river brought these pioneers a day closer to their destiny, and they were anxious to begin the work of realizing their dreams of opportunities to prosper in America.

On November 18, the *Talisman* steamed a few miles up the Ohio River to the trading town of Cairo, Illinois. This trade center bustled with flat boats floating down the Ohio River with hogs and whiskey bound for New Orleans. Carl worked for six hours straight transferring sugar cane and bales of cotton from the Cairo dock. The *Talisman's* cotton was bound for towns east on the Ohio River. Cincinnati, Ohio was a major trade point where cotton was transferred to canal boats heading north and ultimately east to textile mills in the northeastern states.

As he hefted and carried the cotton bales, Carl considered leaving the *Talisman* and booking passage up the Ohio River with the cargo he was unloading. After the storm-tossed ocean voyage and tumultuous Mississippi River expedition for over ten weeks, he thought about land travel in a safe and comfortable train across the western states. But would he arrive in New York earlier by river steamer than going through St. Louis and further by train? By mid-afternoon, the *Talisman* was readied to resume travel back to the confluence of the Ohio and Mississippi Rivers and upstream toward St. Louis. Carl decided to resume his original plan of steamer passage to St. Louis and a railroad ticket to points east through Illinois, Indiana and Ohio.

By nightfall, Carl was bone tired with sweat from exertion dried in his pores. The hard work of being a cargo passenger had both saved him money and let him put his grief energy to a purpose. As he worked, Carl slowly climbed back from the depths of loss to begin a new life without Elizabeth and the children. On this evening, he was one of the first passengers to lay out a blanket and fall into a deep sleep.

Chapter 7
Disaster

The night of November 18 faded into November 19. Churning clouds hid the stars and a three-quarter moon reducing everything on board the *Talisman* to edgy black. Passengers followed their evening routine of toileting and washing, to the extent feasible, with the wavering glow of two kerosene lanterns. Finally, families settled down to sleep on blankets spread on the main and lower decks.

From his familiar floor space near Johann Entz, Carl dreamed of his past life. His dreams began with his marriage to Elizabeth and leaving home several weeks earlier to cross the ocean to America. More vivid than his waking day had been, Carl relived his journey aboard the *Yorkshire*. He heard Dorothee's giggle as he tossed her in the air and David's gurgle of laughter. Elizabeth was at his side watching him play with their children, but in this dream she was silent. The images were no longer in color, and the voices of his father and mother faded in and out of hearing. Then Liza smiled gently from downcast eyes before she turned and disappeared into mist.

Gradually, the numbness that surrounded his heart had begun to subside. He had begun to accept the tradeoff of painful loss that now intertwined memories of his former family life.

A jolt to the *Talisman* rolled Carl against the sidewall of the steerage deck. Just as suddenly, he was awake, sitting up. For a moment the blackness gave him a sense of being lost, out of place. Mr. Butler rang the bell cord from the pilothouse sounding the piercing signal bells, announcing a clear and present danger. As others awoke and cried out in fear, Carl came wide awake. The jolt had come from the front of the steamboat followed by the sound of water pouring into steerage. "Johann, Johann, where are you? We must take everyone up on deck. The steamer is taking on water," urged Carl. "Bring them to me and I will lift them up the ladder."

Johann found his children and handed them one-by-one to Carl who lifted them up through the opening to the main deck. He counted the children, one-two-three-four...seven, eight. Next, Anna, Johann and Carl climbed the ladder. The children cried out, "Papa, Mama, I'm wet and cold...I'm scared...Where are you?" The deck had begun to slope forward toward the source of the river water rushing around them. First the main deck tilted slightly, then more steeply.

Johann directed, "Hold on to me, hold on to Mama or Carl. And pray...Oh, God..." Those were his last words before he lost his footing and scrambled to cling momentarily to the wooden side rail. "Papa...Papa...Three young ones dug fingers into their father's jacket and neck as the rushing blackness dislodged his hands from the railing, and they slipped below the surface of the river together.

Passengers screamed, "Help, help!" in a mad scramble to avoid the fate of others going below the surface of the rushing, churning river water. Anna screamed in desperation, "Johann, oh, God...help me." In a moment, she, too, slid with two of her children toward the swirling blackness and slipped out of sight. In less than six seconds, Carl's friends and dozens of other steerage passengers had screamed, struggled and slipped away from the tilting *Talisman*.

Darkness accentuated the dire circumstance of the *Talisman*.

Within minutes of the collision, most passengers and crew, including the captain were in the water. Some of the victims clung to floating cargo and debris that bumped into them until these small bits of hope became water-logged and sank, too. In their final moments, Johann, Anna and their children flailed desperately, splashing and gulping water in a futile attempt to keep from drowning. In spite of their best efforts, their woolen clothing had become heavily soaked and swiftly pulled them into the deep. What was at first a cacophony of screams and moans diminished, faded away and became an eerie silence. Only the deep throbs of the *Tempest* steamer remained—the heartbeat of the night. Carl's heart sank as he realized Johann, Anna and their children had perished in the crash.

Carl focused on the laboring throbs of the *Tempest's* steam engine's boilers immediately in front of the *Talisman*. Turning to the sounds, he saw the lights of the larger steamer as it turned back to be closer to the anguished cries from the crash point. The *Tempest's* crew threw ropes in a desperate attempt to reach down to rescue survivors of the crash. One of the young Germans who had been rescued was now walking around the deck of the *Tempest* staring at the river, wringing his hands in distress. He called out to his wife and children, as if his protestations could restore them to his side.

A few others tried to stay on board the *Talisman* as long as possible. Mr. Butler, who had been on watch at the wheel, seemed frozen in place. From his vantage point in the pilot house, he could see the steamer sinking rapidly; they were doomed. A deck hand shouted for him to come down repeatedly. They were sinking, but he refused to leave his post until the water was up to his waist. By then, it was too late to for him to save himself, even if he had been able to swim. He was washed backwards by the force of a thousand gallons of plunging river water into the machinery of the engine room and he drowned with his riverboat.

In the churning, frigid November river water, his own survival now seized Carl's attention. The Mississippi River was swift and wide. He had never learned to swim in Prussia where natural water was seldom warm enough to try. Clearly, from the dying silence, most passengers and crew had drowned. And there was little light in the pre-dawn hours to guide survivors to safety.

When Carl's head bumped into a clump of wooden debris, he desperately grasped its oily surface. Carl had time to fill his lungs with air before he lost his hold and slipped beneath the surface of the water. The river water pressed upon his lungs as the weight of his woolen jacket pulled him further down toward the muddy river bottom. His lungs were a few seconds from collapsing under pressure and exhaustion. From deep in his body and soul Carl felt the instinct to survive focus his thoughts. He shed his damning coat and boots allowing his body to rise toward the surface. He pushed arms and legs down on the water enough for his head to finally break the surface of the river. When his hand brushed a floating chunk of the wooden side and railing of the *Talisman*, he reached and grasped as if to life itself.

Carl's scrap of wreckage bobbed like a leaf on a stream. A small, makeshift raft from the side of the steamer had become Carl's lifeboat amidst a profusion of floating bits of a demolished steamer and the wreckage from many lives. To his surprise, another passenger clung to the opposite side of the haphazard raft. Fate had thrown their lots together.

Carl caught his breath and noticed several small rowboats had emerged from shore. His hopes soared when an oarsman rowed quickly toward the disappearing *Talisman* in the light of a kerosene lantern held high by a second boatman.

At first, the few remaining struggling passengers and crew of the *Talisman* called out for rescue. Carl's companion from their makeshift raft held up his hand and shouted, "Help! Help! Over here!" To his horror, Carl witnessed the scoundrels in the rowboats reaching for suitcases and parcels of cargo. Rather than helping drowning passengers climb aboard their rowboats, the ruffians were capturing the spoils from the river disaster. Between Carl and the eastern shore, a thief lugged a wooden trunk onto his boat. It was about the same size and shape as the one Uncle Gottlob had made for Carl's family before they left Sulingen.

Carl and his fellow survivor clung tenaciously to their wooden "lifeboat." They instinctively moved legs and arms to propel themselves toward the safety of the shore. The physical exertion eventually yielded movement of their sagging bodies in the direction of the eastern shore, about 30 yards away. They were desperate to advance out of range of being accosted by the river thieves. This maneuver also shifted them too far away to be rescued by the crew of the *Tempest*.

Carl felt more alone than any time since his loss of family in New Orleans. He was alone in a foreign land. There was neither a person to help him, nor anyone with whom to share the aftermath of the disaster. And he was in the company of a stranger. He knew not whether the stranger would help him, harm him or stand by as passive witness in the case of a threat to Carl's life.

At this moment, Carl's survival rested solely in his own hands. Would he sink into despair, give up and die in moments? Or would the anger in his belly at this calamity, at the storm that blew the *Yorkshire* off course, at the smallpox that took his family, at the desolation of being an immigrant in a foreign land bring forth the energy to escape a watery grave? Balanced between life and death, Carl felt the urge to live surge to his arms clinging to the chunk of wood and his legs weary from pumping. More than the anger and loneliness, Carl simply wanted to live. Life itself urged Carl forward more than anything he had ever wanted in his life. With this realization he summoned the courage and strength to continue making crude strokes toward the river's eastern shore.

In a few more exhausting minutes, the two survivors were close enough to touch down in the muddy bottom of the Mississippi River's eastern shore. Their slogging steps sank ankle deep in brown muddy muck. Each foot stuck to the mud until sucked out through sheer strength and will. Finally on shore, they fell to the ground panting and coughing up muddy mucus and river water. In the first light of dawn Carl breathed a prayer of thanks for surviving the disastrous collision between the *Talisman* and *Tempest*. Then grief for the loss of Johann and Anna Entz and their family melted into his deep feelings of the loss of his own family.

When Carl's gasps for air returned to normal, he sat up. His eyes met those of the man who shared the life raft. "Guten morgan," Carl said cautiously, not to attract notice from the thieves. He had noticed this man on the steamer and thought he was English speaking.

"Hello, I'm Leland Hensley," replied Mr. Hensley in English. "It's a terrible shame the *Talisman* went down. All those people, all that cargo. Such a loss."

"Ja, it is bad," replied Carl. He understood some English, but could only speak a little. "Sprechen sie Deutsch?"

"I speak less German than you speak English," replied Mr. Hensley. "Where are you going? Were you getting off at Cairo or going all the way to St. Louis?"

"I'm going to New York. You?" asked Carl.

"Me? I'm headed to St. Louis for business, then across country by train and down to my home in Kentucky. Now that I'm this far up the Mississippi River, I might as well see if another railroad might get me home any quicker. You're welcome to come with me," Mr. Hensley offered.

Carl paused for a moment while he thought about the wisdom of joining this stranger on an unknown journey. "I need some boots," Carl remarked.

"I'm walking to Cape Girardeau, find some breakfast and check for trains going east," Mr. Hensley stated. Carl hardly noticed when Mr. Hensley withdrew from the Mississippi River bank. He was lost in his own thoughts of the collision.

The river was now calm where the *Talisman* had crashed into the *Tempest*. Glancing to the left, Carl could barely see the *Tempest* disappearing around a bend and out of sight. Then Carl noticed a slow movement, an object arising from the water. The faint silhouette of a horse emerged from the river about 30 yards downstream. Once on shore, she wheezed and coughed to catch her breath from the great exertion of swimming through deep water with a burden in tow. To his surprise, a man followed the horse walking through the slogging river mud. The man had survived the collision by holding the horse's tail and letting the horse tow him to shore. Carl recognized the horse and his owner as the morning sun shone through the river willows. He and his horse had been on the *Talisman*, traveling back home to Cape Girardeau. Both man and mare gasped and heaved to recover breath. After a few minutes' rest, the man said, "Guess I'll ride her home to Cape Girardeau, just up the road." He mounted his mare and twisted his fingers around and through the long hairs of her mane. Turning the mare's head toward the dirt road that ran parallel to the river, he cantered toward home, about a mile away from the sight of the crash on the Mississippi River.

In the collision, Carl lost more than friends and acquaintances, a job with passage to St. Louis. His family trunk was gone along with all of his possessions from the old country and his life with Elizabeth. He survived with only a shirt and his woolen pants. Even his boots were missing, kicked off to aid his clumsy efforts to swim to shore.

Carl bowed his head in sorrow for the loss of so many lives in the crash, especially Johann, Anna and their children. They were gone without notice by anyone but himself. Perhaps he would write a letter to their home town of Olmstead, Prussia as he did not know where they planned to settle in Missouri. The first light of morning revealed a deceptively calm river washing over the lives and dreams that had perished in the night. Carl fell asleep from the emotional and physical exhaustion of swimming to survive the collision.

Carl awoke to the luminous sun crawling up the eastern horizon. For a moment his thoughts were thick with sleep. With movement of his legs to stand, pain from exertion returned Carl's thoughts to the crash of the *Talisman* and the *Tempest*, his escape on a makeshift raft with a fellow passenger and crawling through the mud to the river's shore. His fellow survivors were gone. He was alone.

The scavenger thieves lived on this eastern side of the great river. Under the cover of darkness, they had not noticed Carl come on shore. Now he was exposed in the light of day without boots, food or weapons for protection.

Carl turned away from the river and scrambled up the bank to a grove of beech trees. Underneath and behind dogwood shrubs, Carl felt safe from discovery by the plundering scoundrels. Carl's emotions took him to a place where he had never been. Carl felt a profound, overwhelming anger rising from deep within.

Everything of his old life was lost. He had lost Elizabeth, his two children, the immigration trunk from Uncle Gottlob, even his waistcoat with the last of his few gold coins and his boots.

Carl pounded the earth with his fists in sheer despair at the unfairness of his plight. Why had he survived when so many others had perished? At that moment he wished he was with Liza and his children. The enormity of his losses overwhelmed him with grief and sadness and tears moistened the earth as he pounded down his anger and fear.

Carl questioned his decision to immigrate to America. If they had stayed in Sulingen, Elizabeth would be alive...But other horrible things may have happened.... The fact was, only his determination to survive had endured the crash. As the sun rose over Carl in the beech grove, he acknowledged the enormity of losses from his old life. With this truth in his soul Carl resolved, with God's help, to begin his life anew.

Carl could have stayed hidden all day waiting for cover of darkness except for nagging hunger pangs. Instead, he slipped away from the beech grove to the deeply rutted road coursing parallel to the Mississippi River. He walked barefooted, upstream toward Cape Girardeau.

Later he would read newspaper accounts of the collision and marvel at the details of this enormous tragedy, the collision of his steamboat, the *Talisman* with another steamer, the *Tempest*.

The Talisman*

Before daylight on the morning of November 19th, 1847, the steamboats Talisman *and* Tempest *came in collision of the Mississippi river, half a mile below Cape Girardeau. The* Talisman *was struck forward of the boilers, and sunk within ten minutes. The* Tempest, *which was but slightly damaged, rounded to, and came to the relief of the* Talisman's *crew and passengers. The officers and crews of both steamers exerted themselves to save life and property; but to the disgrace of human nature, it is related that a number of heartless and conscienceless scoundrels came in small boats to the scene of the disaster, and totally regardless of the supplications of the drowning passengers who implored their aid, they betook themselves to plunder, seizing on the floating baggage, and every other article of value which came within their reach. One of the villains engaged in these nefarious operations was a resident of Cincinnati, and bore the name of Barnes. His Christian name, (if he ever had any,) is not mentioned, or gladly would we give it to the public; still more gladly would we "Place in every honest hand a whip to lash the rascal naked through the world."*

Several of the crew and many of the deck passengers were drowned. Two or three families of German emigrants, numbering about twenty-five persons, were among the passengers. Ten persons, all of one family, were lost. An effort was made to rescue the bodies of the persons drowned by means of the diving bell. A young German, who was unable to speak a word of English, continued to wander about the deck of the Tempest, wringing his hands and making exclamations of distress; his eyes were fixed upon the river, as if he expected the deep waters to give up the wife and children they had taken from him. The fate of Mr. Butler, the engineer, was particularly distressing. He was on watch, and although he saw at once and was told repeatedly that the boat was sinking, he refused to leave his post until the water was up to his waist. It was then too late to save himself, and, being unable to withstand the rush of water, he was borne back among the machinery, and drowned.

An interesting young married couple, whose names were unknown to the people of the boat and to their fellow passengers, was among the victims of this calamity. The young gentleman was a good swimmer and might have saved himself; but perished in a vain attempt to save the life of his bride. These two were the only cabin passengers lost; all the rest of the drowned were deck passengers, or persons belonging to the boat. Fifty-one persons, men, women and children, are known to have been drowned by this accident, and probably as many more who are not designated in the annexed list.

Persons known to have been drowned.—Mrs. Nicholls, Mrs. Keziah Bennett, Sarah Bennett, her daughter, aged ten years, Belinda Bennett, another child of Mrs. Bennett, aged eighteen months, Thomas Bennett, aged eight years, and Frances Bennett, aged six years, also children of Mrs. B., Miss Charlotte Cady, Miss Eleanor Cady, Eliza Stone, aged two years. (All of these were from Morgan County, Ohio, moving to

Schuyler County, Ill. They were travelling under the protection of John B. Stone, whose little daughter was lost with the rest.) E. Williams, Johnson O'Neil, deck-hands from Pittsburgh; John Thomas Butler, chief engineer; two children of Mr. Thomas Pryor; sixteen German emigrants, whose names were not entered in the books ; nine negroes belonging to Mr. R. R. Buchner, of Calloway County, Missouri; two young men from Armstrong County, Pa., and a family of ten persons from Illinois, names unknown.

An intelligent man, who was one of the survivors, stated that the deck was crowded with passengers, and the boiler deck was so thronged with passengers, freight, and live stock, that he (the narrator) could scarcely find a place to lie down. He estimated the number of deck passengers at one hundred and fifty, and supposed that half of them, at least, were drowned. Only four or five bodies, among them the two children of Mr. Pryor, were recovered by means of the diving-bell. Mr. Cady, the father of the two young ladies mentioned in the foregoing list, used many efforts to recover their remains, but did not succeed. It is conjectured that most of the bodies were carried to a great distance by the current.

*Lloyd's Steamboat Directory and Disasters on the Western Waters, Cincinnati, Ohio: James T. Lloyd & Co., 1856

Chapter 8
The Ohio River

Carl followed twin ruts that carved a rough, dusty road generally north parallel to the river. He knew the Mississippi River on his left sliced the continent in half, top to bottom. From the hilltop above the river, Carl surveyed gently rolling hills, wooded with black hickory, winged elm, spicebush and sycamores. At the top of the first rise of the road, morning smoke spiraled from a frontier cabin five miles on the southeastern horizon.

Carl had never seen such an expanse of land with so few hints of human habitation. Fall colors of hardwoods, just past their crimson and jonquil peaks, dazzled his senses. But the vastness impacted him the most. The apparent emptiness of his surroundings accentuated his aloneness. Without even boots, much less any kind of weapon, Carl felt more vulnerable than at any other time of his life. His every sense attuned to signs of human or animal presence.

Carl proceeded north on the road along the Mississippi River as quickly as his wounded feet would allow. Every step seemed to tear minute bits of flesh from the tender soles of his feet. Carl formulated a plan of escape if he were to meet anyone on the road. With each bend and summit, he recalculated hiding places and escape routes from a happenstance encounter with predator or scoundrel. A rustle of crisp leaves in the woods to the right halted his trek. As near to noiselessly as possible, Carl moved off the trail and crouched behind a clump of shingle oaks. For a moment, nothing disturbed the silence. Then rustling continued and came closer until Carl saw birds he had never seen in Prussia. A flock of wild turkeys marched regally across the road in single file. Relieved, Carl returned to the trail and gingerly made his way to the top of the next rise.

After an hour on the road, the frontier trading town of Cape Girardeau came into view high above the cliffs on the far, west side of the Mississippi River. A three-level riverboat and numerous steamers were anchored at the base of the far cliff. In contrast, a few smaller flatboats, keels and steamers, clustered around a makeshift dock on the eastern shore. Hoping for food and boots for his blistered, bloody bare feet, Carl limped toward a small general store and livery stable near the eastern dock of Cape Girardeau.

Carl hobbled across the beaten path, up two steps to the front porch of the general store. As he stepped across the threshold, he was greeted with, "Howdy, mister. Kin I hep yuh find what 'cha need?" coming from the scrawny, whiskered general storekeeper behind a wooden counter. Shivers of pain from the pads on his feet and a wave of relief coursed throughout his body

"Guten morgan, my name is Carl Tangeman. I nearly drowned when my boat collided with another boat in the river," replied Carl, using gestures to explain his predicament. He had only scant understanding of the words of the skinny man, a few inches shorter than himself.

"What do yuh need? What do yuh want to buy?" the man asked again, with an inquisitive raise of an eyebrow as he gestured to the goods in his store.

This time Carl understood the intent of the question, if not the actual words. He pointed to his feet, "*Lederstiefel*, bitte." Carl smiled in relief to see the merchant understood and wanted to help him.

The storekeeper shuffled to the back of his store. In a moment he returned with a pair of tall boots with stiff, thick leather sure to protect his feet all winter. Carl slid his weary feet into the boots. "Do they fit 'cha all right?" asked the shopkeeper.

Carl shook his head, took off these boots and indicated a smaller pair was needed. The next pair was a decent fit with a pair of thick wool socks. Carl smiled his approval. Then his mood shifted to a quizzical scrutiny. How could he pay for the necessary boots and socks now that all of his possessions, including his waistcoat with coins from Germany had washed away?

"My name is Miller. Sam Miller," the shopkeeper said, pointing to himself.

Carl repeated, "Sam Miller. Herr Miller."

"Yup. Are you German?"

"Ja, I came by ship to New Orleans."

"This country is fillin' up with Germans," Miller commented. He started for the back door and pointed for Carl to follow him. In back of the rough log structure was a wood pile, higher than his head. With gestures he showed Carl he would trade the boots for Carl splitting and stacking the pile of wood. And Carl could sleep in his cabin that night.

Carl marveled at his good luck. He could work to pay for the boots, and he had a place to sleep out of the weather tonight. Back inside, Carl put on his new socks and boots. Miller gestured to the pot of stew on the potbellied stove. Carl smiled, "Danke." For the rest of the day, the sound of firewood split the air. By evening, Miller's logs were split and stacked and Carl had paid off his new footwear.

Carl and Miller finished the venison stew for supper. Miller asked how Carl lost his boots. He explained with gestures and meager English how the two steamers had collided the night before, many were killed and he lost his boots and waistcoat in the river. Miller took a liking to his foreign visitor and offered him work the next day in exchange for food and sleeping accommodations, a new shirt and overcoat. Carl accepted Miller's friendship and offer to work.

By the third day, Carl's feet were nearly healed. He was ready to leave this oasis of friendship and kindness to resume his journey. Carl chose from three possible routes to progress toward New

York. He could continue his trip by steamer north to St. Louis and board a train east to Chicago and beyond. Alternatively, he could book passage south on a flatboat to Cairo, Illinois, then east by train or river steamer. Finally, he could strike out by footpath east through the dense woods, hoping to avoid miscreant thieves, hungry predators and unpredictable natives. The prospect of river travel was not appealing in the aftermath of his close brush with death in the collision, but it seemed safer than an overland route he knew nothing about. And he could work as a cargo passenger, earning his passage on the Mississippi and Ohio Rivers. Without money for a train ticket east from St. Louis, the river route was the best alternative to make progress toward New York.

On November 22, 1847 with his fresh clothing and new boots, Carl bid his new friend farewell, "Danke, Herr Miller, for your help when I came out of the river."

"Carl, you're a good man. Good luck findin' yer brothers. And remember, keep the sun over yer right shoulder and eventually you'll come to the Atlantic Ocean," Mr. Miller said as he shook hands with Carl and waved as he ambled toward the Mississippi River.

At the east dock, Carl found a flatboat ready to launch downstream toward Cairo with wheat and pork to sell. William Byer, the proprietor, was willing to take Carl on board in exchange for his labor.

The trip back down the Mississippi River to Cairo took one day by flatboat compared to part of a day upstream by steamer. The owner of the flatboat was a farmer from Illinois about Carl's age. He had been on the river for three days before he took on Carl. Every year in the fall, he built a flatboat and loaded it with crops. He could make quadruple the money he would make selling in St. Louis if he could get his goods safely to market in New Orleans. With Carl on board, they took turns at the pole, steering to avoid roots and wreckages. They needed to be near the center of the river to avoid most of those obstacles, conspicuous evidence of the river's reputation as a bad luck highway. Several times, they steered closer to the bluffs and cliffs on the west bank to avoid collisions with upstream vessels.

On Tuesday, November 23, William Byer's flatboat arrived at the sprawling docks of Cairo, Illinois. Both men poled their craft up the Ohio River until they came to a gap in the crowded pier where they landed the flatboat. Upstream and downstream humble keelboats, home-made john-boats, mackinaw with masts, sails and poles, working steamers and handsome showboats drew close to the lengthy pier on the Ohio River side of town. Behind the pier a continuous levee framed the town of Cairo.

"Carl, will you stay with the boat while I look for goods to sell downstream?" Byer asked with words and gestures. After the exhausting task of poling the flatboat upstream to the pier, Carl nodded, thankful for the time to rest and take in the sights.

In short order, Byer returned with fresh bread, cheese and beer. They ate heartily. Byer said, "I found some chickens to take down to New Orleans. When you're finished, come with me and we'll load 'em on the boat."

The two men walked back and forth the 20 feet, reloading 28 squawking crates of hens. With the job finished, they shook hands and Carl struck out on his own to find a cargo ticket for passage eastward up the Ohio River.

"Going east, cargo passenger?" he pointed and asked in his best English as he passed keelboats and steamers offloading and reloading new parcels of cargo. About a block up the levee, two fellows were loading over one hundred bales of cotton. When the shorter boatman flicked his wrist in Carl's direction, he picked up a cotton bale and fell into line with the other two. In an hour he had a job on the keelboat being towed by the steamer, *Rochester*, toward Cincinnati.

The Ohio River was the largest tributary to the Mississippi, about half as wide. Steamers, keelboats and flatboats moved much closer together up and down the smooth stretch of water above Cairo. In the continuous commercial parade, agricultural goods floated toward lucrative trade in New Orleans while steam power brought cotton and passengers and a smattering of products to points of manufacture in eastern cities.

Free from the need to guide the keelboat by pole, the two boatmen relaxed against the cotton bales. The taller one glanced at Carl before he pulled out a jug of whiskey to pass the time until their next stop at Paducah, Kentucky. "Hey, Clyde, have a swig o' lightnin'," he said as he shoved the jug to his companion.

"Don' mind if I do," replied Clyde. The jug was their common interest.

"Hey, you," the tall one grunted to Carl. "What's your name?"

Carl was wary of the two drunks who shared the keelboat with him. "Carl Tangeman," he replied. Those two words revealed his German language origins.

"He's a kraut!" slurred the tall one. "There's too many krauts in this here country. They speak that ugly kraut language. If they come here, they should learn our language."

The two drank and sang raucous songs long past evening shadows keeping Carl from a deep sleep. He was jolted awake when the tall one tripped over his feet in the darkness. His legs withdrew in an instinctive, reflexive movement. In an instant Carl was wide awake crouching near the edge of the keelboat.

"Where's the kraut?" growled the tall one. "Let's have some fun," he staggered toward Carl's previous resting place. Carl thought he could easily defend himself from harm by these two inebriated boatmen, but their moods and actions were erratic and unpredictable.

"There he is," Clyde pointed. Both of the drunks lunged toward Carl who stepped aside allowing them to stumble and crash to the deck. Clyde came to rest a few feet from the deck's edge.

"You dirty little kraut," Clyde shouted at Carl. Then Carl noticed his companion, the tall one was not so lucky. When he stumbled, he had fallen headlong into the Ohio River. Carl could not swim. He knew he could not pull the man out of the water and save him from drowning. Remembering the chunk of wood he clung to with Mr. Hensley, Carl wrestled a cotton bale to the edge of the boat and pushed it off. He could not see if the tall man grabbed his "life boat" or if he simply sank, never to be seen again. When Carl turned back to Clyde, he had fallen asleep where he landed on the deck. Carl sighed in relief and returned to his own light sleep.

"Hey, kraut, where's my pal, Willie?" Clyde moaned the next morning, as he held his aching head. "What happened?"

Carefully, Carl replied, "He is gone, in the river," gesturing beyond the deck. Clyde dropped his head. Carl wondered: *Was it grief, anger or relief?*

Clyde looked up with an inquisitive, puzzled look that turned into laughter. "That guldurned river rat. What'd he do goin' gittin' hisself drowned? He never was too bright." Carl was relieved Clyde had not attacked him over the loss of Willie. "Kraut, you speak some English?"

"A little," replied Carl. Off and on through the day, Carl and Clyde talked about their families, where they were going, the river, the next river port city. Clyde liked Paducah, Kentucky, their next stop. He grew up in Kentucky and liked the fishing at the junction of the Tennessee and Ohio Rivers next to Paducah. He usually caught bullhead and catfish.

The following day was November 25, 1847. The steamer towing Carl's keelboat docked at the pier in Paducah, on the south side of the Ohio River. Mr. Willowby, the owner of the *Rochester*, checked on the keelboat and found out the tall one had drowned.

"Can't be helped, now," stated Mr. Willowby, a proper English merchant hiding behind a bushy black beard. "See here, kraut, the job is yours all the way t' Cincinnati, if you want it."

"Danke, but I get off the river here," Carl replied. He thought the river had become too dangerous; perhaps land travel would be safe from these river scoundrels. He never looked back.

Sprawling freight houses lined the ramshackle dock at Paducah, Kentucky, the town spawned where the Tennessee joined the Ohio River. With the river behind him, Carl needed a safe place to sleep before he struck off to the east, by foot if need be. He found the only boardinghouse near the river.

Carl bathed, ate, and slept soundly in the upstairs back bedroom. When Mrs. Rollins, the widow-lady proprietor of the Robards Boardinghouse offered to wash and clean his clothes, Carl agreed and decided to stay extra days to acquire provisions and recuperate from the effects of the collision and river travel. He used wages he earned working on the dock to purchase a well-worn fixed-blade Bowie knife, a used Kentucky rifle, a knapsack, hard cheese, buffalo jerky, dark bread and apples for the journey. In three days he was rested, provisioned and ready to move east.

Early on November 28, Carl approached a local raft being readied to cross the Tennessee River, only a hundred yards wide this time of year. The crossing itself would only take 20 minutes carried by the current and poled across by raft men. Again, Carl traded his labor to load and unload the raft for free passage.

On the east side of the Tennessee River, Carl struck a pace moving east on a local byway toward Louisville, Kentucky. Away from the river roar, Carl felt his land legs return. The road was broad enough for two wagons to pass one another without one pulling off the road, then back on again. In the morning sun with few travelers on the road, Carl felt safer than he had since he left New Orleans. His ocean and river misadventures left him grateful for the stability of land travel. And he was confident he could work at towns along the way in exchange for room and board, kill game for food and eventually arrive in New York. In case of trouble he was confident of his skills with the knife and rifle.

Carl was not the only person traveling on foot. Two men approached with stacks of raccoon and rabbit pelts on their shoulders looking to trade them for provisions in Paducah. A family of five was walking up ahead, pulling a small, two-wheeled cart heaped with goods covered with canvas. When he caught up to the family and smiled, the father returned a sour look. The remainder of the day Carl enjoyed the sunshine, forest, creeks and hills as he passed by.

By late afternoon, the crowd had thinned out to one or two people per mile. The sounds of the birds and trickling streams entertained him and reminded him of home in Sulingen. Carl heard the underbrush jostling to his right. He stopped and crouched down to catch a glimpse of the source of the disturbance, a long-eared jack rabbit.

With one shot, Carl had supper in hand. To the right the forest was thick with prickly underbrush, but to the left he sighted a granite and limestone outcrop about 20 yards off the road. A layer of anemic white limestone and speckled granite jutted out over a small clearing. From the black smoke markings on the overhanging rocks, this camp site had been used numerous times in the past. The sheltered cove and limestone outcrop afforded him a dry space, protected from wind and rain. Carl used his flint and steel to start a fire with dry twigs and leaves followed by slender sticks, then white oak branches and finally chunks of logs. He enjoyed a tasty meal of roasted rabbit along with dark bread brought from Paducah. When the fire died down, Carl doused it out with water from the nearby stream and settled down for the night.

Close to dawn, on November 29, Carl became aware of footfalls and loud voices on the roadway he had traveled the previous day. Not all of the words were intelligible to him, but it was apparent, three or four men were angry about something. Carl decided to stay put before he arose for the day. One of the men stepped off the road in Carl's direction to pee and said, "Hey, look at this. Somebody's campin' in our woods." As the four strangers stepped through the undergrowth, Carl came wide awake, grabbed his rifle and stood facing them.

"This here is ourn woods. What ya doin' sleepin' in ourn woods?" the leader called to Carl. He used his own rifle to part the underbrush separating the strangers from Carl.

"I travel to Louisville," replied Carl, trying to sound friendly.

"It don' sound like you from 'round here," said the short one with a reddish beard.

"Ja, I am from Prussia," replied Carl.

"He's a dumb-lookin' kraut," said the leader. "I think he's lookin' fer trouble, sleepin' in ourn woods."

Carl was ready when the big one charged. He stepped aside and pushed his assailant broadside with the rifle into the wall of impenetrable limestone and granite. The other three spread out shouting taunts as they decided how much trouble they wanted to cause. "Hey, Shorty, think you can take us all?"

"Why don't ya jus' git on down the road, out 'a ourn woods," asked the tall, lanky one with stringy, black hair.

"I will leave," replied Carl. The dark-eyed one pulled out his skinning knife, crouched and swung his hand in an arc toward Carl. At the same time, he was attacked from behind with a hand chop at his left shoulder releasing the rifle. He punched back with his left elbow, throwing that one off balance. He backed up enough to brandish his own knife. He didn't want to fight, but he would, if there was no option for his own survival.

"Let's get outta here," directed the big one as he staggered to his feet. "I don' wanna see you on this here road again," was his parting order as he held his bleeding nose for comfort. "And I'll take this here rifle for all the trouble you caused us. Git goin', kraut."

Carl waited until the quartet of adversaries was out of sight and sound to the west before he put his knife down. He moved his shoulder where he had been hit; it was sore but otherwise all right. Carl gathered up his knapsack, coat, and knife. He wanted to put distance between himself and the four troublemakers as quickly as possible.

For six days, Carl trekked east on rutted roads wide enough for a covered wagon or a herd of bison. He saw tracks left by both. Careful to avoid other contacts with strangers, he followed narrower Indian trails used by deer and small animals. Thinking of his long treks in the Prussian woods, he recognized scat of deer, raccoons and rabbits. Oaks and maples were familiar, but some species of trees were not. Over time, Carl crowned several ridges overlooking vast forests in all directions. He could see a break in the forest to the north over the Ohio River. To the east and south three ropes of smoke stretched to the clouds. The late fall colors had faded to waves of soft russets, coppers and bare branches.

On the morning of his seventh day east of Paducah, December 6, 1847, Carl climbed up out of a ravine and resumed his journey east on a deer trail. Within an hour hoof beats sounded behind him. Slipping off the trail, Carl hid behind a clump of red chokeberry brush.

To his surprise, the hoof beats belonged to a riderless roan mare. Carl immediately stepped into the path of the cantering horse. He reached out and grasped the bridle, excited at his good luck. Carl spoke softly as he stroked the mare's nose, neck and back. In less than an hour, Carl had made a new friend and he was astride the mare. He had not been on a horse since working in his father's livery and saddlery shop back in Sulingen.

After a week on his own without agreeable human contact, he talked with the only living creature in his immediate vicinity—the horse he named *Strahlend.*

"Strahlend, my name is Carl Tangeman. I am from Sulingen, near Hannover, Prussia," he began. "I'm on my way to New York to meet my brothers, George and Wilhelm. They must be worried. Maybe they have given up by now. I wrote them a letter, but I don't know if they received it…. My family in Prussia don't know about Elizabeth . . ." Carl broke down and sobbed for several minutes.

"Elizabeth was my wife…Dorothee, my darling daughter, was a young one, just walking and starting to talk…and wee David…. I knew Elizabeth since we were children…in Sulingen. She was beautiful…kind…a good mother. She should not have died……. but she did." Throughout the day Carl allowed his feelings of loss and grief to surface. Memories from Sulingen, their wedding, the births of their children, their decision to emigrate, the ocean voyage, the storm that blew them off course, arriving in New Orleans, the hospital…. Details of his time in New Orleans were fading, but his grief was jagged as a broken knife edge.

When the sun sank below the horizon, Carl was exhausted from spilling the tears of his heart's grief. He could barely dismount, tie Strahlend's reins and drag himself to a sheltering thicket of sycamore trees. He ate the last of his provisions, a dry bread crust, and dropped into a heap on a bed of leaves, covered by his long coat. In the distance, Carl recognized a wolf's call piercing the night as he fell into a deep sleep.

On the new day of December 7, a thin blanket of snow clung to Carl and Strahlend. Carl led Strahlend to feed on patches of grass and berry thickets and drink from the nearby stream before he mounted to resume his journey. On horseback, Carl could cover twice the pace of foot travel. But, where would he arrive at the end of this day? He remembered the advice of his friend, Mr. Miller. Eventually, he would arrive at the Atlantic Ocean if he kept the sun over his right shoulder.

From the top of the next ridge, Carl and Strahlend began a descent downward toward the yellow banks along the Ohio River. Twists and turns, but continuously downward. By afternoon, they could see the river and a village on the southern shore. Carl was exhausted and hunger pains radiated out from his belly.

The Owensborough Livery Stable was on Leitchfield Road, the main approach to the town from the south. Carl needed to sell Strahlend, but he decided to stay at the livery his first night in Owensborough, unwilling to part ways, just yet, with his best friend in America. The equine smells of the stable were familiar, a welcome reminder of his father's saddlery shop and livery in Sulingen. After supper Carl climbed upstairs to the hayloft close to the warmth and safety and company of the twelve horses. He slept soundly to the breathing and occasional snort from his four-legged companions. The next morning, Carl said "good-bye" to Strahlend and pocketed five dollars for the sale. Then he made his way to the small dock near the center of Owensborough.

Owensborough had a dozen steamers in various stages of cargo transfers and preparations to continue up and down the Ohio River. Carl explored the riverfront downstream, then upstream. At the far upper end of the dock, three men were loading a steamer, the *Dauntless*, with grain and corn. "Hey, lookin' for a job?" called the foreman as he waved at Carl.

"Ja, I will help," replied Carl. For the rest of the afternoon and the following day, Carl joined another roustabout from Knoxville and two slaves. At dusk, Carl asked the foreman, "When are you going to Cincinnati?"

"Tomorrow morning, if the fog ain't too thick," replied the bearded, barrel-chested foreman.

By dusk, Carl was spent. He trudged slowly back to his boardinghouse on Front Street. Carl was grateful for a bowl of beef stew and a clean bed.

On December 10, Carl woke up to a steady drizzle, dressed, packed and ate flapjacks and grits for breakfast. A half-hour later he boarded the steamer, *Dauntless*, eager to begin this leg of his journey to Cincinnati, Ohio.

Chapter 9
Cincinnati

Carl boarded the river steamer, *Dauntless*, at Owensborough, Kentucky bound for Louisville, Kentucky and Cincinnati, Ohio. Since commencing this journey up the Mississippi River, Carl had become increasingly reticent to get to know his fellow travelers. They would not be in his life for long, or they might make trouble for him as a German-speaking immigrant. Either way, he judged it best to keep to himself, do his work and stay clear of conflicts. These were his thoughts as he observed more than a dozen passengers walking up the gangplank.

The throbbing *Dauntless* maneuvered upstream in the steady drizzle at a lumbering pace. By noon, they had passed three snarly upturned roots, visible in the winter decline of river depth and flow. Dodging around each one, the captain powered down the throttle as the rain thickened to the consistency of pea soup. Having little to no visibility and mounting chances of being grounded on a root or sandbar, he dropped anchor near the right bank of the Ohio River to wait out the lugubrious storm. The rain alternated between steady downpour and torrential storm, alienating cheerful spirits for the next two days. Carl sighed at the thought the crew members and cargo passengers were stuck with each other until the rain abated.

People slept, lulled by the wind in the sycamore trees over-hanging the riverbank. A deck of playing cards appeared, and games with low stakes or no stakes were played. Carl walked back and forth the covered main deck, fighting the boredom with physical activity. There were several single men playing cards and telling stories near the stern, a few families in the middle along with three middle-aged women. Finally, he sat down near the bow of the steamer, within earshot of a family group visiting with one another.

"Hello, come join us," the father invited. Reluctantly, Carl moved closer, and the man offered his hand, "My name is Lund-quist, Bjorn Lundquist."

"Hello, my name is Carl Tangeman. I am from Sulingen, near Hannover, Prussia," replied Carl.

"Ja? We are from Stockholm. We have been in America since '42. Pardon me, this is my wife, Agnes, and my children Britta, Eleanora and Gerhard. Traveling with us is our friend, Irma Mueller. We are returning from Louisville, Kentucky where we visited family and friends."

"I'm glad to meet you. This is my first winter in America," replied Carl. He was used to a cold, dark winter in Sulingen, but this was his first winter trip on a creaky, drafty steamboat up the Ohio River. The potbellied stove near the middle warmed the main deck—too hot if you were close, too cold from more than seven feet away. Passengers moved to adjust their preferred locations, accordingly.

Carl and Bjorn struck up a friendly conversation sharing details about life in their old countries—wars and famines, revolution and emigration. All the while Carl observed Irma, brown wavy hair, blue eyes, slender frame. She was deep in a conversation with the Lundquist children and their mother. When the children commented about how cold they were, their parents moved them closer to the stove leaving Carl and Irma in the bow seats.

This was the first time Carl had spoken with a young, single woman since he had said goodbye to his beloved Elizabeth over a month earlier. He felt awkward, at first, even out of place. If she had not been engaged to be married, he would have withdrawn to the single men. In this circumstance, his casual interest was not misinterpreted as she was betrothed to another. Under the chaperonage of the Lundquists, both Carl and Irma spoke casually and freely, with the honesty of knowing they would not meet again after this trip.

Carl missed the intimacy of sharing details of everyday life with Elizabeth—the stories of problems overcome and small signs of growth in the children. Just below the surface, Carl felt sadness as he acknowledged that chapter of his life was behind him. Now Irma listened with a genuine interest in his challenges of travel in a new land, what he learned, what he thought about the people he met. She listened like Elizabeth had listened, and their first day on the steamboat passed with restrained contentment.

On the second day Carl drifted from group to group among the passengers and crew. He discovered a couple from Oldenburg, in the old country, Adrian and Inge Muth. They passed a few hours speaking German, remembering the foods, describing their families and friends left behind. Some in their old country were angry and frustrated, and the Muths were glad to escape their negative feelings of hopelessness. Other memories brought tears to their eyes.

On the second day of the storm, Carl and Irma spoke again. They shared their hopes and dreams for the future. Irma told him of Kristof, her fiancé, and their plans for a life together in Louisville. Kristof was learning the lumber trade from his father. He would build a house for them in the spring, and she planned to come to Louisville after her term of teaching was finished in May. Their wedding was scheduled next summer.

Carl told her about the crossing with Elizabeth and the children and their hope for a better life in America. She was the first person he had spoken to about his family and how they died in New Orleans. Tears were just below the surface as he described Sulingen, their wedding, deciding the emigrate, packing the family trunk, leaving Waterloo harbor, the storm, New Orleans, smallpox, the funeral and traveling up the Mississippi and Ohio rivers alone. By the time he finished, Irma felt a deep connection with Carl, a momentary friend she would always remember.

"You must have loved her very much," Irma responded.

"Ja, that is true. Thank you for listening," Carl said. He rose from the bench and returned to the heat of the stove. He felt another page of grieving had been turned during his conversation with Irma.

On the evening of the third day, the temperature fell and the rain became snow. The fourth day began in clear, piercing, bone-chilling sunshine. Temperatures were so low not even direct sunshine relieved the bitterness in the air. The riverbanks were white with snow, and the overhanging sycamores and willows stood still, enshrined in crystal shrouds of ice. Captain Miller began the steam engine, bellowed for the anchor to be lifted and steered his vessel back to the main channel of the Ohio River. All on board cheered while hull timbers stretched and cracked under the strain of lurching forward in the icy waterway. The keel cracked under the strain of breaking ice and scraping a snag in the river.

Throughout the morning of December 14, the captain slowly guided his damaged steamboat safely upstream toward Cincinnati, Ohio. He followed the main channel that veered close to the far left bank and docked at Clarksville, Indiana. Carl could see nothing but what looked like rapids ahead known as Falls of the Ohio. This natural impediment was the most dangerous point in the entire length of the Ohio River. At Clarksville, Captain Miller welcomed a local guide aboard to steer the steamer across the river to the dock at Louisville, Kentucky. The water flow was usually dangerously low in December; only a local guide familiar with the changing dance of the river could accomplish this docking without disembarking passengers and crew, offloading cargo and re-engaging a similar vessel upstream—an extremely costly endeavor.

William Daggett smiled confidently to passengers as he climbed up to the spiral steps to the pilot house where Captain Miller would turn over the wheel. Daggett sighted day-marks (white X's painted on wooden signs on shore) and gingerly inching across the channel and around Corn Island. At last, the *Dauntless* limped into dock at Louisville, Kentucky. Captain

Miller announced the steamer would need repairs to the keel. "In four days we may be able to resume our journey."

Upon hearing news of this further delay, Bjorn Lundquist, on behalf of his family and Irma, negotiated with the captain for partial refund. They booked passage on a different steamer leaving that afternoon, and Carl never saw any of these new friends again.

In Louisville, Carl encountered more Africans than he had seen since New Orleans and Natchez. Much of the hustle and bustle of Louisville was the manifestation of their labor. Cargo was the main trade of the town, and slave labor was used to transport and transfer cargo across town or onto steamers moving up or downstream. An overseer was always present shouting orders and directing each task.

At the dock, dozens of laborers, mostly Africans, were removing debris from a steamer that had gone aground on rocks of the rapids at Corn Island. In the freezing water, pieces of decking, pilot house, guard rails and buckets or paddles from the paddlewheel were lifted and handed one-by-one along a brigade to shore. After five minutes, each worker took one step toward shore, and eventually stepped into a warming shed. After ten minutes, the warmest worker returned to the river to begin the freezing work before he worked his way back to shore. This process continued throughout the day.

Carl perused the town and eventually found an inexpensive boardinghouse where the food smelled good. He booked a room with the money he received for Strahlend. Dinner with the other roomers consisted of roasted duck, potatoes, carrots and apple cake for dessert. He slept deeply, accompanied by comforting memories of playing with Elizabeth as children together in Sulingen.

Morning came drenched in icy rain. Breakfast of coffee, biscuits and sausage gravy gave Carl a hearty start to the day. He walked to the docks and looked for work. He found no jobs as everyone sought shelter from the punishing deluge. By afternoon the skies dried up, and Carl loaded barrels of pork bellies on to a steamer headed downstream. The monotonous physical labor provided time to reflect.

America is a vast country. Carl had been traveling for over a month and he was still far from his goal of finding his brothers, George and Wilhelm, in New York City. The fall had turned to winter, and steamer travel had become even more treacherous. Daily, the pace of travel slowed to a snail's pace, or stopped all together. Carl's former patience had turned to an anxious drive across the countryside. Coming upon Christmas, he was still hundreds of miles from New York. At this rate he would be lucky to arrive in that great east coast harbor city by spring.

The next day rain fell intermittently as Carl lifted, toted and carried barrels, boxes and bundles of goods to and from steamers and flatboats. Rain had soaked the soil of the watersheds for the nearby tributaries of the Ohio. All morning the skies darkened and storm clouds shed their abundance. The Ohio River rose steadily. By late afternoon the Ohio River flowed over the dock, but planks could still reach steamers anchored beside the boardwalk. Steamer captains anxiously directed crew and other laborers to load their vessels before the river obliterated the entire dock area. If the rain stopped soon, this transient high water could be forgotten by Christmas.

The cold, steely rain did not stop. It dripped from leaves, slid down trunks, formed into rivulets, and splashed down ravines filling upriver basins between Pittsburgh, Pennsylvania and Paducah, Kentucky. The unseasonable flood made a moving lake of the Ohio River and dozens of its tributaries. The captain of the *Dauntless* recognized the river was too dangerous to navigate until the flood waters receded. Carl stayed in Louisville for two more days.

Carl's chose Phinneas' Restaurant for his last lunch in Louisville. Carl followed the lunch smells past three slaves lounging on the boardwalk outside. He ducked in and quickly ordered venison stew, and dark bread with salami and cheese.

As he finished, Carl heard a raspy voice shout, "Git yer lazy selves movin'. The General's ready to go." An overseer grabbed the arm of the tall African slave and kicked the shorter one in the leg. Carl did not fully grasp the slave system in America. Whereas he looked for work to support himself, these slaves performed the same type of work without wages.

On December 18, 1847, the Ohio River reached a flood stage of 61 feet above normal in Cincinnati, Ohio. Flooding was similar in Louisville and points in between.

By December 20, the rains had stopped, the river water was receding and, once again, larger river steamers began to navigate the Ohio River. Carl continued his upstream journey on the *Dauntless*. The going was slow. One night the temperature dropped well below freezing, low enough for a skin of ice to change into a thick winter coat by morning. The *Dauntless* moved forward slowly in the daylight, careful to avoid ice chunks poised to puncture the hull.

The *Dauntless* arrived in Cincinnati just before Christmas, December 23, 1847, snow sifting over every person and everything. The snow reminded Carl of winter walks in the forest with Elizabeth and friends in Sulingen even though today it fell on the cobblestone streets of Cincinnati. The memories brought warmth to his heart as he approached this inland city of more than 70,000 people. A crew member mentioned Carl might want to visit a large German section of Cincinnati called Over-the-Rhine. "Head up Broadway to the center of town. Then follow your nose for the best bratwurst this side of New York." Carl smiled his thanks for the directions. He shook hands with his captain and thanked him for safe passage before he set out in search of a warm bratwurst and sauerkraut.

From the pier on the far west end of the public landing, Carl sauntered east along the waterlogged "Bottom" where streets of the city met the wharf. Turning at Broadway, Carl followed the cobblestone street that extended upward toward "the Hill," the name for the commercial downtown of Cincinnati. A few blocks up Broadway, Carl stopped at a dimly lit bar for a break from the snow and to ask for directions to Over-the-Rhine. Unknown to Carl, previous to his appearance the conversation had centered on the steady influx of German-speaking immigrants to Cincinnati.

"They come here for jobs in the meat-packing plants," said a short, English laborer leaning on the polished bar, "but there are too many of 'em."

"Do you know how many of 'em live in one apartment? Dozens. Over-the-Rhine is a terrible part of town," added a taller fellow.

"They want everything to be just like the old country. Don't they know this is America? They should learn English," returned the short one. "They have to have their own newspapers, even German churches and schools. At this rate, they won't ever be real Americans."

"Oh, they want to be citizens so they get the vote. Next thing y' know, they'll want to be the mayor and such. It's a shame what's happening to this town," chimed in a third. The native Cincinnatians felt threatened by the large influx of newcomers who were changing the local flavor and culture of this largest inland city in America in 1847.

As Carl entered the tavern, the three disgruntled English laborers retreated from the bar and slipped out the front door.

"Pardon, can you direct me to Over-the-Rhine?" Carl asked the bartender.

"Sure thing, fella. Go up Broadway, then turn left at Fifth Street. Go three blocks, then turn right. In a few blocks you'll recognize little Germany," replied the bartender as he gestured toward Over-the-Rhine.

The three English troublemakers glanced back to make sure the German speaking stranger followed them up Broadway. When Carl turned on to Fifth Street, they were waiting for him.

"Ned, what d'ya think? Does this guy look like a kraut? Does he smell like a kraut?"

"I'm not sure. Wha'd you think, Tom?" Shorty asked as they pushed Carl back and forth between each other. Carl knew he was in trouble when two men grabbed Carl's elbows. The third punched Carl hard in the stomach. He doubled over and reached for his knife in a sheath on his belt. When he straightened up, he took a slap on the face. Then he slashed at the arm of the closest thug holding his left arm, drawing blood.

"Oh, my arm. I've been cut! Let's get outta here," he shouted. Before they withdrew, one more punch landed with a crack to Carl's ribs.

The taller bully warned, "You better move on. We don' wan' cha here, kraut."

Finally left alone, Carl withdrew to the shadows to catch his breath. Like his movement along animal trails in Kentucky, for the rest of the evening, Carl stayed out of sight when anyone came along Fifth Street. In an hour of slow going he arrived at the edge of Over-the-Rhine, past the Erie and Miami Canal. The fragrances of sauerkraut, pickles and bratwurst extended a cloak of hospitality. He stopped at the first boardinghouse with a light on the front porch.

Mrs. Stolz answered the knock on the door and looked carefully at Carl's bloody lip, limp and how his right arm was bent to protect the right side of his body.

In labored breaths he said, "My name is Carl Tangeman from Sulingen, near Hannover, Prussia. Do you have a room that is vacant?"

She clucked, "Ach, ach. Come in. Ja, I have a room for you."

Carl followed Mrs. Stolz up the stairway to the third room on the left. "Breakfast is at 7 am, dinner at noon and supper at 6. Would you like a bowl of borscht for your supper?"

"Ja, bitte," replied Carl.

Mrs. Stolz returned to Carl's room with a steaming bowl of thick beet soup, "Now, you must rest."

On December 24, Carl slept in. It was a deep, healing sleep, and Carl did not awaken until close to noon. At first glance, he didn't know where he was or how he had gotten there. Where was this small room with its faded wallpaper and lacey curtains? When he tried to sit up, the pain jarred his memory of the mugging by nativists and Mrs. Stolz' welcome to her boardinghouse. He lay back on the pillow, panting. Carl heard steps on the stairs to the second floor landing. Mrs. Stolz was leading a few people and whispering in hushed tones. Carl heard her say, "...safe here...." A door closed softly, and one set of footsteps made their way back downstairs.

Carl moved slowly and carefully to sit on the edge of the bed, and then stood up. He was stiff from the beating. Pains from the injured ribs shot through his body with each breath. In slow, careful movements, Carl found the chamber pot behind the door of the commode and washed up afterwards. When Mrs. Stolz heard Carl move in the upstairs hallway, she called up the stairway, "Mr. Tangeman, wait, I'll bring your tray up to your room." She brought Carl a tray with steaming hot pork stew and coffee.

He slept all afternoon and awakened just before supper. In spite of the pain in his ribs, Carl joined the other boarders for a supper of sauerkraut and bratwurst. Not exactly like his mother's, but when he took the first bite, he felt like he was back home. And he could speak German without fear of retribution by strangers who resented his presence in Cincinnati.

One of Carl's fellow boarders was a physician, Dr. Tanner. "Mr. Tangeman, if you allow me to examine you, I may be able to help heal your injuries." After the examination, he wrapped Carl's rib cage to help his cracked ribs heal. The bandage restricted his breathing. The injury was painful, but not serious. Dr. Tanner recommended a week of rest before setting out for New York.

Carl spent Christmas weekend at Mrs. Stolz' Boardinghouse in Over-the-Rhine. On Christmas Eve, Carl and Dr. Tanner attended a midnight service at St. Matthaeus German Evangelical Church. As they donned coats, Dr. Tanner asked, "Mrs. Stolz, would you like to join us?"

She looked up from her needlework and smiled at the thought of a Christmas Eve outing. "No, bitte, I must stay here tonight," she replied, quickly looking down at the needlepoint frame in her lap. Carl was puzzled by her obvious desire to join them, yet polite refusal to do so. What was so important to compel her to stay home on Christmas Eve?

The small stone church was filled with parishioners and newcomers eager to connect with ancient scriptures, familiar music and comforting Christmas traditions. The popular "Stille Nacht (Silent Night)" had recently come to Cincinnati with German immigrants. Now its soaring lyrics filled the peaked sanctuary with swirling harmonies. The candlelight service was an intimate celebration that reminded congregants of village life with family and friends in the old country. Tears flowed from every eye. The congregation split into four-part harmony as they sang "Lo, How a Rose E'er Blooming," Elizabeth's favorite Christmas carol. The service ended with the German hymn, "O Tannenbaum."

When Dr. Tanner and Carl arrived back at the boardinghouse, Mrs. Stolz served *gluhwein* (hot mulled wine) and *lebkuchen* (spiced cookies) to everyone in the boardinghouse. They talked of Christmases past and their hopes for the future in their adopted country. Carl's memories of home flooded his heart with an ache for all he had left behind and not yet found in his adopted country.

"Carl, have you tried this lebkuchen? It is my mother's recipe. See if you like it," asked Mrs. Stolz. She liked Carl. He did not complain about his misfortune of being attacked by thugs. As he healed, he helped her with chores around the boardinghouse. And he reminded her of her own son, about his age. They became fast friends.

"Ja, *sehr gut*. Just like my mother made back home," Carl replied. He thought back to Christmas in 1846 in Sulingen. Before their decision to emigrate, before his son, David, was born, before conflict had broken out with Denmark, before starvation came to Sulingen. At that time, a Christmas in 1847 alone in Cincinnati, was unimaginable. Carl's attention came back to the boardinghouse, and he joined his fellow boarders as they reminisced over gluhwein and a game of cards.

Saturday, December 25, morning dawned clear with icy wind blowing off the river. Carl bundled up in his leather boots and long coat from Cape Girardeau, ready to explore Over-the-Rhine. In daylight, Carl roamed the streets passing German churches, biergartens, recreation clubs, and small shops with apartments above for owner families. Everyone spoke German, dialects from Berlin to Bavaria, Austria to Olmstead. In one way, he desired to stay in the warmth and familiarity of this enclave of German-speaking neighbors. Only his desire to join his brothers in New York propelled him to resume his journey.

By Monday, December 27, Cincinnati was again humming with the engines of factories, river commerce and trade. Carl ventured beyond Over-the-Rhine to discover the businesses of Cincinnati. On the way he stopped by the Berliner Brewery and

Biergarten, bought one of several German newspapers, ordered a coffee and relaxed to read the newspaper.

At the next table, a young fellow dressed in Bavarian woolens asked, "Guten morgan, are you looking for a job? I know a guy who can use some help."

"Danke, but I will be leaving soon. Did you hear about the wreck of the Stephen Whitney passenger ship off the coast of southern Ireland?" asked Carl gesturing with his newspaper. "The fog was thick and they crashed into the rocks. Those Irish, they will do anything to escape the famine. Are there Irish here in Cincinnati?"

"Ja, ja, some Irish are here, but many more immigrants from Prussia and Bavaria. Sometimes the English give us a hard time. They don't like us very much. They are scared we take their jobs, but we just want to make a living. Times were so hard back home, we had no other choice."

"Ja, immigrants have a hard time before they come and after they get here, but on the other side of the Ohio River, the Africans are slaves. I heard some of them come across the river at night and go up to Canada. How do they escape? I saw the overseers in Kentucky keep them in line. Africans don't get any time to themselves," replied Carl.

"There are some free Africans and white abolitionists who help them cross the river at night. They call it the Underground Railroad," replied the Bavarian. "Then they sneak out of Cincinnati covered up in wagons and stay in 'safe houses' all the way up to Canada," explained the young man. This conversation reminded Carl of the slave markets he had encountered in New Orleans and Natchez, Mississippi.

Carl stood up and folded the newspaper under his arm. "Danke, it was good to visit with you," as he shook hands in farewell and withdrew to the street. Growing weary from his explorations, Carl turned south to find his way back to Mrs. Stolz' boardinghouse. Noticing the alley behind the boardinghouse, Carl turned and walked toward Mrs. Stolz at the back gate. As he approached, a wagon filled with cargo pulled away from Mrs. Stolz who quickly dabbed her eyes with the edge of her apron. "Oh, Carl, you're back."

"Mrs. Stolz, is something wrong? Can I help in any way?" Carl asked. Carl recognized the stoic countenance with emotion seeping around the edges of ice blue eyes, a look he had seen in his home village whenever trouble fell on friends or family members. With much to bear, they tried to protect others from their own pain. He placed his hand gently on Mrs. Stolz arm and led her back into the boardinghouse.

"It is nothing to do with you. Some things are difficult, and I try to help when I can," Mrs. Stolz stated without really explaining the difficulty. She looked into Carl's eyes and saw understanding, and she decided to risk explaining about the wagon.

"There were people in the wagon, moving north out of Cincinnati. An African woman and her four children were staying here for the past five days. They escaped from their slave owner and crossed the Ohio River as soon as the flood waters subsided last week. This house is part of the Underground Railroad."

Carl knew African slaves escaped across the Ohio River. He had only heard the term, Underground Railroad, earlier at the biergarten. He did not know what the slaves did once across into the free state of Ohio. "You are brave to offer shelter to Africans seeking their freedom. Why must they hide?" asked Carl.

"In slaveholding states like Kentucky, they are considered property. If they escape, their owners have the right to recapture their 'stolen' property, even in a free state like Ohio. It is a terrible law. The only option is for Africans to be smuggled all the way to safety in Canada. The family in the wagon had a sick child, the two-year old. They could not stay here any longer, but they are in great danger traveling with a sick child," explained Mrs. Stolz.

Carl knew first-hand the feelings of loneliness and uncertainty while traveling through a foreign land. "Carl, would you like to stay in Cincinnati? It seems you have abolitionist sympathies. Would you like to help in this work?" asked Mrs. Stolz. She was at risk as she asked Carl to join the work of the Underground Railroad. If he turned her in to the police, he could claim a reward of several hundred dollars.

Carl was silent for a few minutes while he considered staying in Cincinnati, finding a job and helping his new friend. He agreed with her; slavery was a dishonor to those enslaved, the owners and those who stood on the sidelines. He admired her greatly for taking the risk to help Africans escape to freedom in Canada. And Mrs. Stolz' boardinghouse was the first place he had felt safe and really at home in America.

As strong as these feelings were, he longed to see his brothers again. "I'm sorry, Mrs. Stolz. I must continue my journey to New York to join my brothers. Thank you for trusting me with your secret. I will never forget your kindness to these Africans and to me."

Chapter 10
Eastward to Pittsburgh

On Thursday, December 30, 1847, Carl packed his satchel and enjoyed his last breakfast at Mrs. Stolz' boardinghouse. He felt nearly healthy, except for the lingering ache in his ribs, as he sauntered down to the Cincinnati public landing. Mrs. Stolz had suggested the steamer, *Convoy*, owned by her friend, if it was back in Cincinnati. On the boardwalk, Carl stopped to buy a newspaper from the newspaper boy, to learn of the wars in Europe and happenings in America. Within the hour, Carl had found the steamer, *Convoy*, loaded with cotton bales pointed upstream.

The small cargo steamer had a crew of three in addition to Carl: the captain, Hans and Fritz. Much to his surprise, Hans and Fritz had a German shepherd named Stein. Carl leaned over and patted Stein, scratching behind his ears. Unlike his experiences between Cairo, Illinois and Paducah, Kentucky, this crew was friendly and they didn't get drunk. Carl settled in for an uneventful, even enjoyable, passage to Pittsburgh. Hans and Fritz had come from Rhineplatz in 1841. They took Carl under wings of friendship sharing stories of being newly minted immigrants, naturalization, and river politics.

"Everybody wants to make money on the river, shippers, farmers and merchants. But nobody wants to fix the river," lamented the older man, Hans.

"The states along the river need to work together and all help to pay for the dredging and construction. One state always holds back. Then Congress doesn't want all the other states to pay for something they believe will only benefit a part of the country," added Fritz.

"Just like Prussia, the different states always fighting amongst themselves," laughed Hans. "Last year the river was low in the Falls of the Ohio. Boats ran into rocks and roots all up and down the river. Someone needs to dredge the river, but no one is doing it. Do you see that there snaggy sand bar?" he asked as the small steamer veered to the left around a large sand bar, just beyond the mouth of the little Miami River.

Carl commented, "There are other obstacles in the river, too. I was in a collision between two boats on the Mississippi River. My boat sank to below the surface. Another steamer could easily smash into it now and suffer damage or worse."

"This river needs to be cleaned up. That's for sure," continued Hans. "The other problem with the river is the flooding. Every few years watch out for a rainy spell upstream like the one before Christmas. The river was a lake for several days. Now the Ohio is back within banks, for the most part."

"That was a bad 'un 'fore Christmas. Especially downstream from Cincinnati," added Fritz. "The riverbanks got soggy and slid into the river. Look at that..." he said pointing out fresh cuts into the riverbanks. Rounding a curve in the riverbank, a scene of ruin appeared on the left bank. The debris line left by the overflowing flood waters rose and disappeared behind river willows on the eroded bluff.

"The town hall of Utopia is now that shambles of stones and timbers!" exclaimed Hans pointing upward to the left bank. "It's one of those 'utopian' communities, a 'perfect' place to live."

Fritz explained, "A few years ago, a Frenchman came and set up a communal society. He believed there would be 3,500 years of peace, and the Atlantic Ocean would turn into lemonade."

Laughter ensued. "When neither of those happened, the community broke up. Last year Mr. Wattles bought the town, and his spiritualists moved the town hall to that spot near the river. There was a newspaper article about what happened on December 13. While they held a party in the new town hall, the flood bore down on the town hall, destroyed its south wall and swept away most of the people," related Fritz. "All that is left is the stone foundation and part of the walls."

"I heard about bodies drifting down the river but never saw any," said Hans.

"The flood was destructive down past Louisville, too," commented Carl.

As the sun slipped behind river bluffs, the steamer captain ordered the anchor to be dropped near Mechanicsburgh, Ohio.

In the morning mist of December 31, 1847, the steamer shuddered and throbbed to life. The steamer moved toward the center of the river where swifter waters broke up the thin, icy crust along the river's edges. By the middle of the afternoon, the *Convoy* was churning steadily upstream at eight miles per hour when Hans shouted, "Look what's in the water. Never seen such a thing." As if he understood the words, Stein looked over the railing and sniffed at the rippling river. Suddenly, Stein leaped off the starboard side of the steamer in a splashy arch.

"Hey, Stein. What are you doing? Get back here!" shouted Hans. Swimming lightly in the water, Stein clamped his jaws on the back of a fat black squirrel and swam back to the vessel. He looked up at Hans who reached down to grab the dead squirrel. "Ja, ja, we will have squirrel stew for supper," Hans chuckled. In less than an hour, Stein had captured eight more squirrels and delivered them to Hans. "Now, how are we going to bring you back on board, Stein?"

Fritz replied, "Come Stein, come, come." He extended the rescue pole down to Stein, hooked his collar and pulled him up to the lowest level of deck at the stern. Stein panted rapidly from the exertion and cold. He shook his fur, sending river water droplets that landed in a wide circle.

Carl helped dress the squirrels and drop them in the stew pot. A few potatoes and onions later, the stew was simmering deliciously.

The journey's tedium was relieved by stops at small towns that clung to high bluffs. In Manchester, Ohio, two passengers, a couple moving back to Steubenville, Ohio, boarded the *Convoy*. The woman was seen sniffling, on the verge of tears most of the day. She revealed they had lost everything in the recent flood-waters. Their dry goods store had been inundated by over four feet of water ruining most of their merchandise. They sold the few goods untouched by the dirt-soaked torrent to buy tickets to travel back to her parents.

The next port of call was Portsmouth, Ohio, a larger town at the mouth of the Ohio and Erie Canal connecting the Ohio River with Lake Erie. Over 4,000 inhabitants supported shops, a post office and printing shop, as well as the surrounding farms, river and canal traffic. In Prussia, Carl remembered a canal was built to connect the North Sea with the Baltic for defense pur-poses. Here in America the canals seemed to be built primarily for commercial purposes, to transport goods to market.

The three workers aboard the *Convoy* unloaded most of the cotton bales at the port of Portsmouth. "Why are we unloading the cotton here?" asked Carl.

Hans explained, "We leave a lot of cotton here. It gets loaded on steamers going up the canal to Lake Erie, over to the Hudson River and down toward New York. From there, it is shipped to textile factories in Connecticut and up the coast."

"Is it a shorter route to New York?" inquired Carl.

"No, it's much longer. The shortest way to New York is through Pittsburgh, then over the canal/train route to Philadel-phia and by steamer to New York. And they need a lot of workers loading and unloading cargo going through Pittsburgh," contin-ued Hans.

After a long day of exhausting work, Carl, Hans and Fritz walked along Front Street looking for a restaurant with an inviting aroma. Unlike his experience being assaulted alone in Cincinnati, Carl relaxed in the presence of fellow German speakers. After supper, the men found a boardinghouse with rooms for all four. They visited with the other boarders in the evening that marked the end of 1847, the most fateful year of Carl's life. As they toasted the New Year, Carl felt sadness for the loss of his family, yet hopeful he would join Wilhelm and George soon.

By morning, Carl was refreshed from a warm bath, sleeping in a clean bed that did not move and breakfast of thick bacon slices, corn meal mush, homemade corn syrup, fried apples and coffee.

Back on the river, on January 1, 1848, a thick fog forced the *Convoy* to stay at anchor an extra day. When the sun finally cleared off the mist the following morning, the small steamer moved out to the main channel. Within minutes, they nearly clipped a "pirogue" or dug-out canoe. It was so heavily loaded with parcels, the boatman had difficulty peering downstream. "Hey, Mister, move to the side," gestured Hans as he tried to help steer the *Convoy* away from the canoe using long poles. The captain used a jackstaff (a tall pole mounted on the bow of the steamer) to judge the distance to steer a straight path toward a far point on shore. Meanwhile, Carl waved arms widely indicating the canoe should move toward the northern shore. At the last moment, a strong keel stroke on the right pulled the canoe out of collision range with the larger vessel.

By late afternoon, they passed the cliffs outside Hanging Rock, Ohio. Cut away by erosion of floods and the normal passage of downstream flows, the cliffs were a sheer drop of 100 feet or more from the grassy cap to sandy mud beach at river's edge. Burlington, Ohio was a convenient anchor point as the day turned to dusk.

Dawn came late on January 3, tucked into folds of relentless ice and fog. Stein was the only creature with a coat suited to dwell within a cloud. The humans felt the chill down to the marrow in their bones as they huddled in the cabin. All of that day and the next, the *Convoy* remained at anchor near Burlington. Crew and passengers, alike, were relieved to be on their way the following morning. Through light mist the *Convoy* maneuvered around the island at the mouth of the Big Guyandot River on the

Virginia* side of the Ohio River. That evening, Fritz dropped anchor at the request of the captain at Gallipolis, Ohio.

Upstream from Gallipolis, both sides of the river were wooded with silver maple, honey locust, sycamore and black oak, thick enough to hide a black bear even in the winter. The bare and leafless deciduous forest was punctuated by small towns and occasional smoke from log cabins in the woods. Carl deduced that farms were much larger with cabins much further apart than in the old country. Were the settlers lonely, living so isolated from neighbors? Coming from village life in Prussia, Carl had lived close to family and friends his whole life. Even army life was a communal experience. America was a vast territory, sparse and desolate beyond European imagination.

By late afternoon, the *Convoy* was in sight of Parkersburg, Virginia. The captain eased the steamer to the right up the Kanawha River to the wharf on the left. Parkersburg was built at the mouth of the Kanawha flowing north from Virginia into the Ohio River. Given the recent flooding and wet season, a considerable flow was coming down the Kanawha slowing down the progress of *Convoy* into a docking station. River water lapped within a foot of the dock. Finally, the steamboat was secure, and Carl, Hans, Fritz and Stein disembarked.

"Enjoy your time ashore," called the captain. "I need you back by seven in the morning."

"Ja, Ja. We will be here," assured Fritz. They walked along bustling First Street where warehouses overflowed with lumber, coal, wheat and whiskey. The wharf was crowded with people, rich and poor, African and white, young and old. Unlike other stops along the Ohio River, the unrest in the crowd was palpable. Eyes seemed to dart every direction in search of danger. Numerous armed men patrolled the wharf.

Carl asked, "What is the trouble? Why are there so many armed men in this town?"

West Virginia was part of Virginia until it separated during the Civil War, 1863.

Leaning toward Carl, Hans replied, "Bounty hunters. They're lookin' for runaway slaves. Do you see the flyers they hold? They have descriptions of run-away slaves from further south. If a bounty hunter catches a slave and returns him to the owner, he receives a reward. Catching slaves pays well."

Inside the hour, the three immigrants found rooms at the Garfield Boarding House on Garfield Street. Stein was allowed to stay with them if he did not disturb the other guests.

The three German steamer crew members were back at the *Convoy* early the following morning, "Good morning, men. Unload these crates of dry goods and take them to that warehouse," directed the captain pointing to the end of the pier.

By mid-morning, the cargo was unloaded and the captain invited, "Now, come on board," to a young overseer with two Africans in tow. They hung their heads as they shuffled on board behind him. "In three hours, we will stop at Vienna, Virginia to offload cargo. And we will take on coal, cheapest port on this stretch of the river. Barring trouble of any sort, we will anchor down tonight near Marietta, Ohio."

The overseer gestured for the two to sit on the deck near the bow of the steamer. Each had a thin jacket and their feet were wrapped in rags for minimal protection from the winter damp and cold. The overseer sat a few feet away, watchful of his two charges as he observed the other travelers.

The *Convoy* moved toward the main channel of the Kanawha River past an island and sandbar on the left. Back on the Ohio River, the steam engine labored upstream.

Sunshine and gentle breezes allowed Carl and his fellow travelers to be in the open air most of the day. The overseer and his two charges did not move from their self-assigned seats. A pointed object, perhaps a weapon, protruded from the overseer's pocket. He kept his right hand in that pocket.

As Carl observed the three new passengers, he noticed a subtle change in their behaviors. The Africans seemed to relax, heads not so bowed. They exchanged a few inaudible words with each other. The overseer kept a steady gaze out of the steamer to other river vessels and sights along the shore.

By early afternoon, the small town of Vienna, (West) Virginia came into view, a few houses, general store and a small dock. As they pulled in close to the meager dock, the overseer withdrew the weapon from his pocket. Simultaneously, the two Africans assumed their previous hunched over postures.

As if on cue, three lanky backwoodsmen stepped out of the underbrush with shouldered rifles. They strode toward the modest steamer, "Got any darkies on this here vessel?" the obvious leader shouted to the captain. Stein came to attention, ears pricked forward, hair standing on end along his back, a low growl forming in his chest.

"Oh, just a couple of Africans with their overseer, goin' to do a job in Marietta. So they tell me," casually replied the captain. The worried threesome remained mute in a practiced display of relaxed demeanor. The overseer met the eyes of the locals in a steady gaze, revolver splayed casually across his lap. Time was suspended while the locals decided whether to try to board the steamer to examine the Africans or not.

"Ah, heck. Be on your way. We was lookin' fer a group of four Africans said to run away 'bout 50 miles yonder south o' here," decided the leader. He and his two companions stepped back from the dock, gave one last curious inspection of the Africans and shuffled on toward the general store.

Hans gestured to Carl to help carry crates of dry goods to the dock and heft boxes of coal on to the steamer. In short order the delivery was made, coal was replenished and the *Convoy* released from its mooring. Crew and passengers leaned back and relaxed from the tension of facing down the bounty hunters. They entered the Ohio River across from Vienna Island.

Out of sight of Vienna, Carl cast a quizzical look to Fritz who explained, "Those despicable fellows were after runaway slaves. There's good money for returning a slave to his owner."

"But these two are not slaves, or are they?" asked Carl.

Hans glanced rapidly from Fritz to the captain who gave a slight nod and back before he replied, "This steamer is part of the Underground Railroad. We deliver African slaves from Parkersburg, Virginia to Steubenville, Ohio. With so many bounty hunters trying to catch runaways, now we provide escorts who act like overseers. This is John Gibson, a Quaker from Mount Pleasant, Ohio. He appears to be mean so the Africans have good reason to keep their heads down, harder to recognize." John nodded in acknowledgement of the introduction to Carl.

Carl was relieved, "That's why everyone was tense. Have you ever been caught transporting Africans?"

"I haven't been caught, but others in our group have had close calls," replied Fritz. "My 'packages' have always been delivered safely."

Hans related, "One time near Cincinnati, I was helping a group out of a boat that had brought them across from Kentucky. They barely made it to a shack by the river for shelter when a couple of policemen came along with a lantern. We said we were setting night lines for fishing, and they believed us. If they had discovered our Africans, they would have been sent back to their slave owners for a bounty of $200 each and we would have been arrested."

Carl pondered this revelation and then asked, "Are you friends with Mrs. Stolz in Cincinnati? I stayed at her boardinghouse."

"Ja, she is part of our group. She has helped more than a hundred people with shelter and food before they continue on their way to Canada."

"That must be why she suggested this steamer for the river journey to Pittsburgh. I discovered her sending a family away in a wagon. She was upset because a small child was ill and she was worried the family could be discovered if the child cried out. Then she told me of the Underground Railroad, and I assured her I supported her work and would keep her secret." Hans and Fritz smiled, grateful to be assured Carl was a co-conspirator.

As the *Convoy* came in sight of Marietta, Ohio at the mouth of the Muskingum River, the captain steered to the left and dropped anchor in a protected cove. "We will stay on board tonight, stop at the dock in Marietta tomorrow," he announced. Carl joined the rest of the group in the head house, protected from a biting, wind-driven sleet. They ate dried out bread and beans for supper.

"Weigh anchor," called the captain on January 7. Hans complied, turning the crank to raise anchor and free the *Convoy* to continue upstream.

"What is that structure?" asked Carl, referring to a fortification unlike any others in Marietta.

"That is an Indian town of some sort," replied Hans. "No one lives there, but they did many years ago. Now it is a curiosity, and the town of Marietta grew up around it."

To minimize their exposure to bounty hunters, the captain kept the *Convoy* in the river channel in the day, secluded coves at night. They dropped anchor near Sistersville and Elizabethtown, Virginia on their way to Steubenville, Ohio, their next stop along the Underground Railroad.

The *Convoy* maneuvered among dozens of watercraft along this portion of the Ohio River. Handmade keelboats, majestic paddlewheel riverboats, as well as some steamboats and barges, floated in a majestic cargo parade downstream toward New Orleans. Steam power was required for the upstream progress. Past Elizabethtown, a bevy of steamboats towed open-decked coal boats upstream, stopping to resupply steam vessels who hailed their help. It saved time to be resupplied in mid-stream, but the coal boat captain charged accordingly.

The *Convoy* paused at anchor for an infusion of coal. "Carl, tie this cordelle line to the horn of the cavel." A metal shank was used to attach the mooring line to the adjacent coal boat. With the *Convoy* and coal boat steady in the moving water, a wooden trough was laid between the full coal bin and the empty coal box. Finally the coal chute door was lifted, and the coal rumbled down the trough.

While the coal refuel was underway, the Africans' escort stayed in his role as overseer—a mean look, weapon suggested in his pocket. The slaves lowered their heads, cowered in the presence of the overseer. They repeated this charade whenever passing another river craft.

On the approach to Steubenville, Ohio, the captain steered

to the right across from Wells Run on the left. He veered to the right even further to capture the river channel and to avoid a large sandbar. Just beyond the small tributary from Ohio, large flocks of merino sheep grazed across the low bluff on the left. "Ah, sheep," commented Carl. "These are the first sheep I have seen in America." He smiled enjoying the sight and the memories it evoked: sheep grazing in hillside pastures, sheering sheep, carding the wool, and finally, socks and sweaters knitted by women and some men in Sulingen.

"Steubenville has a large woolen mill. Their woolen goods are the best in the country," added Hans. "They also have a paper mill, a cotton factory and two breweries."

"The Steubenville beer is different from the old country, but tasty," laughed Fritz. "I could use one about now." He knew the *Convoy* would be tied up overnight at the Steubenville pier. John Gibson left the river with the two Africans headed toward their next safe house further north on the way to Canada. Meanwhile, Fritz, Hans and Carl walked along Water Street past the warehouses and bars. They turned left on Market Street, walked three blocks past city hall on the right and stopped for *spätzle* and *wiener schnitzel*.

The following morning, a heavy, cold mist shrouded the river, preventing safe travel up the river. By the time the mist lifted, the temperatures had dropped to single digits and the Ohio River froze over. It was three days before temperatures rose enough for the river ice to melt and the river to become passable.

On January 10, 1848, just beyond Steubenville, the *Convoy* came upon a 60-foot keelboat with an enclosed cabin listing hard to the right. Cargo had spilled off the deck and was floating downstream. Three men were using poles in an attempt to right the loaded homemade keelboat bound for New Orleans. The local farmers had gambled they could travel during the dead of winter when prices were at their highest. If the boat could not be set upright, the cost of the boat, the crew and their goods would be lost. "Need a hand?" shouted the captain as the *Convoy* came close. "We could send you a line, thread it around that tree on shore and then pull you upright."

"Much obliged. Toss me the line," returned the keelboat crewman. Fritz unwound more than enough line and tossed the weighted end to the keelboat. The shortest boatman caught it, climbed overboard and clambered up the shallow bank. When the line was around the stout tree, he brought the end back to the keelboat, and then tossed it back to the *Convoy*. Missing on the first toss, the keelboat crewman unwound more of the line and Hans caught it on the second try. The captain turned the *Convoy* bow to shore and put it into reverse in the lowest gear. Slowly, the steamer moved backward and simultaneously righted the keelboat. The boatmen poled mightily and succeeded leveraging their keelboat into the main channel and a cheer went up from crew in both vessels.

Above Steubenville, for the remainder of the day, the *Convoy* dodged among ice floes barely avoiding the fate of the keelboat they had helped earlier in the day.

Chapter 11
Over the Allegheny Mountains

January 19, 1848
Sulingen, Hannover, Prussia

Dear Papa and Mama,
    Greetings to all of you from Pittsburgh, Pennsylvania. It has been a long and dangerous journey since I last wrote to you in Natchez, Mississippi. The trip continued up the Mississippi River for several more days. Many details are lost to me as I was in the depths of grief and despair after Elizabeth and the children died of a fever in New Orleans. Through the kindness of strangers, many of whom were also German-speaking immigrants, I made the journey up the Mississippi River past Memphis, Tennessee and Cairo, Illinois.
    On November 19, 1847, before the sun came up, my vessel, the Talisman, *was struck by the steamer* Tempest, *as it journeyed down the Mississippi River. The* Talisman *sank within a few minutes taking*

127

most of the passengers and crew down, too. I was lucky to grab onto a large piece of wood from the steamer and swim in my clumsy way to shore. At that time, I only had the clothes on my back. My boots I kicked off in the river and, the trunk from Uncle Gottlob was lost in the crash.

Now I am in Pittsburgh, a city in the hills of Pennsylvania. Tomorrow I will continue this journey to New York. Between Pittsburgh and Philadelphia is a series of canals and railroads. In four days I will travel 400 miles over the Allegheny Mountains. I have been told it is a frightening way to travel, but it will save a few weeks time to arrive in New York.

Here in America there is something called the Underground Railroad. It is a network of people who believe slavery is wrong, and they help Africans escape from their slaveholders. Others called bounty hunters attempt to recapture runaway slaves and return them to their masters for a reward as much as $500. The tension was high along the Ohio River which is the division between slave holding and free states. Please pray with me for the safety of slaves escaping to freedom and those who assist them.

My heart is heavy, still, with grief and loss, but the thought of reuniting with George and Wilhelm sustains me on my way to New York.

Please share my love and well wishes with Wilhelmina and Louisa. Elizabeth's family is in my prayers, too.

With gratitude and affection from your son,

Carl
Pittsburgh, Pennsylvania

Carl arrived in Pittsburgh, Pennsylvania on January 18, 1848 at the headwaters of the Ohio River. He saw the Allegheny River on the left and Monongahela River on the right as they flowed together to form the Ohio River at a triangle of land where the city of Pittsburgh was established many years earlier. The captain steered the *Convoy* to the right of the point of land between those two rivers. Carl noticed new docks stretched a half mile along the right side of that point of land. "Why are the docks so new?" asked Carl. "Is this a new city?"

"No, Pittsburgh has been here for a century. Three years ago a fire got out of hand on the docks. Burned up most everything in the point. The docks were rebuilt last year," replied Fritz.

Behind the docks Carl noticed the commercial district of Pittsburgh, evidenced by smoke stacks, church spires and commercial buildings. Further upriver the Smithfield Street Bridge spanned the Monongahela River. At the Pittsburgh docks Carl left Hans, Fritz and Stein to continue his journey to find George and Wilhelm in New York on his own.

It was a kind farewell. Carl helped load the *Convoy* with coal for their return trip downstream to Cincinnati. He would always remember the kindness of Fritz, Hans, Stein and the captain, as well as their work to help slaves escape to freedom on the Underground Railroad. "I'm looking for the fastest way to New York. Do you have a recommendation?" Carl asked.

"Ja, do you see that bridge over the river, up ahead?" replied Hans. "That is the Smithfield Bridge. Beyond the bridge, turn left on Smithfield Street. Go about a mile or so until you see the overhead aqueduct. It's part of the Pennsylvania Canal. There are places to stay along the way. I have stayed at Pittsburgh Boardinghouse and Hendrix Boardinghouse. They will give you directions how to secure passage to Philadelphia."

"Danke, danke! And good luck delivering many more packages," Carl said as he shook hands and bid farewell to his steamboat friends. They shared a friendship much deeper than he had anticipated.

Alone in the western Pennsylvania coal and iron town of Pittsburgh, Carl found accommodations at the Pittsburgh Boardinghouse on Smithfield Street. It was within walking distance of the Pennsylvania Canal and Allegheny Portage Railroad. Carl considered his other option to take a canal north to Buffalo, New York then across New York state on the Erie Canal to Albany, and finally on the Hudson River south to New York City. The canal and portage route was more than twice as fast as going through Buffalo. In about four days, he would be in Philadelphia. In another day, or so, New York.

Carl walked along the docks and Smithfield Street. Remembering his encounter with thugs in Cincinnati, Carl kept to himself the entire mile weaving among dock workers carrying the goods of trade. Before nightfall he found the Pittsburgh Boardinghouse and a room with Mrs. Bittleman, a jovial woman in her fifties with a thick German accent. "Ja, I have a room for you. Are you hungry?" she asked. "*Buttermilchsuppe mit speck und zwiebeln* will be served in an hour."

Carl felt at home immediately. As at Mrs. Stolz' Boardinghouse, speaking his native German brought a sense of trust and safety. At supper, Mrs. Bittleman asked, "So Carl, where are you from?"

"I'm from Sulingen, near Hannover, Prussia. I have been in this country since November. I come from New Orleans, on my way to New York," replied Carl.

"It is a long way from here to New York. Have you traveled by yourself from New Orleans?" asked Klaus, an immigrant from Bavaria. Carl mused to himself, he had already come so far. Certainly, he could complete another few hundred miles.

"Yes, I have been by myself. Sometimes it was easy, other times the language was difficult. Now I need to get to New York the shortest way. My brothers are waiting for me there. My friend on the steamer said the Pennsylvania Canal is the best way to get over the mountains...," said Carl. The room erupted in laughter.

"Wh-what's wrong?" asked Carl, unsure how to respond.

Mrs. Bittleman explained, "There are high mountains between here and Philadelphia. A canal takes you to Johnstown. Then you will be on a train to the top of the mountain and down the other side. The train is pulled by cables up the mountain on inclines. Very steep, very scary. In Holidaysburg you will go back to a canal and finish your trip in your canal boat attached to a train car," she laughed from her belly.

Klaus added, "You get to Philadelphia in four days, but four frightful days they are!"

Carl sat back in his chair, sharing the laughter. He hoped these acquaintances greatly exaggerated the train experience, but he couldn't be sure until he climbed the mountains himself. He spent the evening with Mrs. Bittleman and her boarders speaking his native tongue, sharing news from home and tales of life in their adopted country.

———◦◦◦———

With clean clothes and a rested body and soul, Carl left Mrs. Bittleman's establishment at 8 am on January 19, 1848. He saw horses canter up Smithfield Street, snorting and snuffling clouds of warm breath cooled in the damp, frigid air. Carl passed the William Penn Hotel on the right and entered a "hole-in-the-wall" newspaper shop two doors down. He purchased a tourist pocket map of Pennsylvania for the remainder of his journey across the state. Across the top of the map was a profile illustration of the Pennsylvania Canal with insets of coal regions near Philadelphia, Lehigh and Schuykill.

Carl walked to the small basin at Second Avenue and boarded the *Molly G.*, a canal boat. He purchased a ticket for the Pennsylvania Canal and Allegheny Portage Railroad on board the broad, flat canal craft. With all passengers on board, horses pulled the canal boat via aqueduct across the Allegheny River. Carl could hardly believe he was crossing high above a broad river through a water-filled trough. He had heard of aqueducts made by the Romans nearly two thousand years earlier, but this was the first one he had seen in person. It was another unexpected experience to have in America.

Carl was surprised how much faster a canal boat could move compared with the laborious steamers navigating upstream among other river vessels, large and small sandbars and snags of tree roots and stumps. Rather than a steam engine, the lighter weight canal boat was pulled by teams of horses trotting along paths parallel to the canal. It was an altogether different experience: quiet, smooth and fast up to the base of each lock.

Carl carefully observed how the canal boat maneuvered through the mechanism of the lock. These structures were designed to raise the *Molly G.* up the grade of the terrain in successive stages. He watched in fascination as the canal crew, closed gates, pumped in water to raise the water level and opened other gates at the higher level. At the higher level, fresh horses were hitched to pull the *Molly G.* forward at a surprising pace of up to 15 miles an hour.

Although the day was chilly, at first, most of the passengers preferred to be outside watching their craft maneuver the locks. The first few locks held their attention as evidenced by exclamations of, "Look, the gate moved into place," and "The water is pouring in. We're moving up." It was a marvel few had seen before. When the horses again took up the task of pulling the canal boat, the brisk breeze and beginning drizzle sent most of the passengers into the cabin. But Carl turned up his collar, pulled his duster coat close around his neck and stayed on the open deck. He took in each step of the process of entering and leaving locks, raising and lowering gates. He was determined to learn all that he could about the operation of the lock machinery.

On this first day of their journey to Philadelphia, the *Molly G.* progressed through several locks and arrived in Johnstown, Pennsylvania. They stayed overnight in Johnstown House, a small hotel built to serve passengers on the canal boats. In the evening Carl explored the coal town strolling past the market and through the neighborhood where the miners lived in small wooden shacks.

On January 20, the *Molly G.* left Johnstown bound for the five inclines that would lift the canal boat to the summit of the Allegheny Mountains. At the base of the first incline, the canal boat entered a hitching shed. First the horses were unhitched from the side cleats. Next the steel cables were fastened to the *Molly G.* In this way the *Molly G.* was floated onto railroad cars riding the rails for the portage over the mountains. Finally, the stationary steam engine at the top of the incline pulled the cable taut and drew the railroad car upward to the top of the incline.

In the hitching shed at the top of the incline, the railroad car was disconnected from the cable, floated into the canal and hitched to a fresh team of horses. The horses pulled the canal boat swiftly through the canal to the base of the next incline where the entire process was repeated, five times in all on the west side of the summit.

The second night was spent in Cresson, Pennsylvania at the Samuel Lemon House, a tavern near the halfway point between Johnstown and Holidaysburg, Pennsylvania. Although it was a small, remote borough, there were comfortable accommodations, a satisfying venison stew and freshly-baked daily bread.

Waking to snow on the ground the following morning, Carl and his fellow passengers shivered until they gathered in the cabin on board the canal boat and felt the warmth from the bodies of fellow passengers. Carl thought back to descriptions of the trip over the mountains and smiled inwardly. Surely, those he met at Mrs. Bittleman's had simply exaggerated to share a moment of levity. Thus far, he was fascinated with the intricate machines that controlled the locks and inclines. The journey felt much more like a holiday than a frightening experience; even their destination on the far side of the mountain was named Holidaysburg.

About four miles east of Johnstown, the horses and canal boat entered the Staple Bend Tunnel under a rounded, stone archway. The clip-clop of the horses' hooves echoed through the darkening tube while drips of limestone water from the ceiling plopped on the cabin roof. The passengers shivered in the darkness, eager for the first glimmer of light to appear in the distance.

Emerging from the east end of the tunnel, Carl saw an immense ocean of forests in all directions. He was again struck with the enormity, the vastness of his adopted country. In spite of his losses, disappointments and grief since leaving Sulingen, this trip was changing Carl's heart and mind to imagine new possibilities— ideas he was anxious to share with his brothers in New York.

Soon the *Molly G.* approached the hitching shed of the first downward incline. Again, they entered the shed, traded the leather straps of the horses' harnesses for the steel cable attached to a stationary steam engine at the top of the incline. Slipping over the upper edge of the incline, the steam engine lowered the *Molly G.* slowly by controlling the force of gravity. Women swooned; men looked anywhere except down the mountain. Carl felt light headed, knowing he was completely at the mercy of the cable pulley system. Instinctively, he clutched the brass rail enclosing the cabin with white knuckles stretched to the point of pain by his grip. He cringed with the screech of metal rollers, and now understood the dour predictions by his fellow boarders in Pittsburgh.

The remainder of the inclines left Carl breathless, exhilarated and acutely conscious of the knot of anxiety in the pit of his stomach. Upon completing the fifth incline on the eastern side of the mountains, passengers relaxed and shared their mutual relief for a safe trip over the Pennsylvania Canal and Allegheny Portage Railroad.

From Holidaysburg, Carl's canal boat continued to the borough of Columbia through numerous locks. At Columbia the canal boat was transferred to a railroad flatbed car and secured by cables. Carl and his fellow passengers walked to the passenger cars at the front of the train where they rode in relative indoor comfort. In a matter of hours, the *Molly G.* with all passengers arrived safely in Philadelphia, Pennsylvania. The railroad station was the hub of railroads from Baltimore and Reading, moving coal from the mines to cities up and down the east coast.

Walking out of the Philadelphia Railroad station, Carl brushed snow flurries out of his face. As in other cities on this trip, Carl found a boardinghouse a block away. The bed was lumpy and the food was plain, but Carl was rested by the next morning. He was up early, anxious to begin the last leg to complete his journey from New Orleans to New York. "Mr. Tangeman, be sure to see our Liberty Bell, better than anything you'll see in New York. It's down t' Independence Square," Carl's fellow boarder pointed down the street, downhill toward the river.

"Danke, it will be a pleasure to see the bell that rings for liberty in America," replied Carl.

Carl examined his pocket map to see the miles he had already come. He realized he was only a few hours away from New York.

Against his heartfelt preference, Carl secured passage on the *Washington* of Swiftsure Transportation Line, a Steam Tow-Boat Company between New York and Philadelphia, via the Delaware and Raritan Canal. It was a cargo vessel, and again, Carl exchanged his labor for a cargo ticket. Confident this would be his last trip over water for a very long time, Carl was eager to begin and end the journey to New York.

Along with two other boats, Carl's canal boat was towed by a steamer down the Delaware River to Bordentown, New Jersey. At the dock, Carl and three crew members unloaded boxes and barrels of dry goods. Within an hour they were again being towed, this time on the Delaware and Raritan Canal. Along the canal, small farms and towns were spaced much closer together than those he had seen west of the Allegheny Mountains. Smoke curled from chimneys, farmers split wood and delivery wagons were loading goods from canal docks. Carl was curious to see how people in these more settled areas lived. He was especially interested in the crops being grown, animals and tools being used. As it was winter, he found it difficult to determine the crops that had been harvested the previous fall. The orchards looked to have plentiful apple trees as had been the case in Sulingen, too. He saw corn shocks and corn cribs on several of the farms, too.

About half-way along the Delaware and Raritan Canal that paralleled the Delaware River, Carl saw the borough of Princeton on the left side of the canal. Narrow spires and towers of the town and Princeton University showed through and above clumps of bare-branched hardwoods. At New Brunswick the *Washington* canal boat was towed into the channel of the Raritan River. In less than an hour Carl's craft was in Raritan Bay sliding past the borough of New Dorp on the left. His pocket map showed they were over half-way from Philadelphia to New York harbor, and Carl watched anxiously to catch first sight of the city of New York.

On the north edge of Raritan Bay, the Hudson River flowed through the Narrows from New York Bay where tenement houses, towers and church steeples came into view. Carl was overcome with joy and relief. One of Carl's fellow passengers smiled at the sight, "Ain't it great to be home?"

His companion replied, "Ja, ja, 'tis a fine sight, if you don't mind livin' in a stinkin' tenement house. I thought America was the land of opportunity. All I got is work 'til I drop and another mouth to feed every other year. Sometimes I wish I was back in the old country."

Carl would not let this fellow's sour mood spoil his buoyant spirits. Even as the gray skies spit daggers of arctic wind out of the north and his steamer with canal boats in tow passed Governor's Island, Carl yearned for the city where his brothers lived.

Chapter 12
George and Wilhelm in New York City

On June 23, 1847, Wilhelm stopped at the New York Post Office on his way home from work. With letter in hand, he ran back to the apartment and took the steps to the third floor two at time. "George, a letter from Sulingen! It is from Carl. He and Elizabeth and the children are on their way to New York. They will arrive in November," exclaimed Wilhelm, breathless from running. He read the letter aloud to George as he paced and nearly danced across the apartment floor.

This was the best news imaginable from the old country. At last they could make plans to find the land they needed to begin producing crops. (*Chapter 1, letter from Carl, May 10, 1847*)

"The apartment is big enough for Carl, Elizabeth, Dorothee and David to stay for a while, until Carl gets a job," added George his mind leaping forward with plans. "Ships arriving and departing at the Brooklyn Harbor always need men to load and unload cargo. We will introduce him to the foremen we know." They knew Elizabeth could help them make their apartment into a fine, orderly Prussian home and the little ones would liven up their lives.

"Or we could all move west right away," responded Wilhelm. "We will see what Carl wants to do when he arrives."

"I will write a letter back to Carl and Elizabeth to let them know we are here and ready to welcome them to America," said George. (*Chapter 1, letter from George, July 5, 1847*)

George and Wilhelm were anxious to share all they had learned and accomplished in New York with their only close family members likely to emigrate to America.

━━━━━◦◦◦◦━━━━━

Each day in November, 1847, George or Wilhelm Tangeman stopped at the Liverpool Dock Office on the East River on their way home from work hoping for news of their brother's packet ship, the *Yorkshire*. They found where new arrivals from Liverpool were assigned to dock. Had the *Yorkshire* docked that day? Had it dropped anchor nearby? The answer from the harbormaster's office was the same every day, "Sorry, no sign of the *Yorkshire* today."

By November 25, George and Wilhelm still hoped for a joyous reunion with Carl's family in New York, but their hopes were beginning to fade. They both looked up to Carl and respected his successful army service. Even though George and Wilhelm were much younger than Carl, they had grown close to him working together in the woodworking shop and helping their father in the saddlery business. His confidence and encouragement greatly influenced their decision to emigrate to America; this last year in America heightened their desire to be together again.

The Tangeman brothers knew Elizabeth well and liked her very much, and they were eager to see their young niece and nephew. As with every visit to the New York Post Office, they longed for news Carl and Elizabeth would bring from their family and friends in Sulingen.

━━━━━◦◦◦◦━━━━━

December began in icy rain, and it became much more difficult for George and Wilhelm to maintain hope. Each succeeding day of December arrived and receded along with the brothers' hopes for the survival of Carl, Elizabeth and the children. They knew ocean travel was risky from the stories of shipwrecks retold in immigrant circles. Some ships were known to have sunk in a storm. Others ran aground at low tide. Others simply vanished, never to be heard from again. Although they continued to work courageously for long hours in miserable conditions, their efforts to maintain optimism faltered and their hopes diminished to the point of disappearing all together.

By Christmas Eve, George and Wilhelm knew there was very little chance of ever seeing their brother and his family again. On their way home from the Liverpool dock, the drifting snow carried their thoughts back to Christmases in Sulingen, singing, laughing and enjoying sweet bread, cakes filled with candied fruits, and lebkuchen. George spoke first, "The time has come to accept the truth. Carl and his family are lost. It is no use waiting and hoping their ship will arrive in Brooklyn Harbor. It has been too long since they left Bremerhaven for them to survive the ocean journey."

On the verge of tears, Wilhelm replied, "You're right. We may never know what happened to the *Yorkshire*.... What should we do?" A few minutes passed as George and Wilhelm each struggled with unavoidable emotions of loss and grief. Anguish overcame their natural reserve, and the brothers clung to each other for a few moments in a desperate embrace.

"If we were back home,..." began George, momentarily indulging in second guessing the decision to emigrate now that Carl was not here to share their new life in America.

"But we are here," said Wilhelm. "Life will be difficult to imagine without Carl and Elizabeth, but we must find another future in America."

George recovered from his momentary indulgence of an emotional return to Sulingen. "Carl would say it is time to make our own plans to move west. Are you ready to do that?" he asked. "Let's go for a walk to clear our thoughts." As the brothers walked through Kleindeutschland, they resisted the holiday atmosphere of gluewein booths selling warm spiced wine and

Christmas goods available in *Christkindl markt* stalls. Much like Christmas at home, the fragrance of lebkuchen and bratwurst sausages filled the streets.

Seemingly without forethought, the brothers made their way on the familiar route that led from the harbor. "George, it's Christmas Eve. Would you like to attend a Christmas Eve service?" asked Wilhelm, remembering the Deutsche Evangelische Reformiert Kirche they had attended a few times. It was on their way to and from work on the harbor each day.

"Ja, I would do that. We may not have a German church where we are going out west," Wilhelm responded as he led the way down Madison Street to the intersection with Montgomery Street.

The two young Prussians entered the small sanctuary, removed their hats and looked for vacant spaces in a nearby pew. The lifting interior spaces reminded them of their Sulingen Kirche. George thought of Carl's wedding to Elizabeth in their home church. Their daughter, Dorothee, was baptized in the same church before her uncles left for America. George wanted to write to his parents about this candlelight service, their last time to attend before they moved to Ohio.

The congregation had already begun to sing the first hymn, "O, Tannenbaum." Halfway down the center aisle, George and Wilhelm slipped onto a pew next to an older couple and joined the hymn. As the congregation began the last verse of this familiar Christmas song, the organist ceased his accompaniment, allowing the four-part harmony of robust and lyrical voices to lift and reverberate in the stone bound spaces. George bowed his head to conceal the tears of grief for Carl's family and memories of those they left in the old country.

Steeped in reminders of their Sulingen Kirche, George and Wilhelm finally relaxed and soaked in the music and scriptural Christmas story. The last hymn, "Silent Night," was sung in a cappella four-part harmony in the German tradition.

Following the service, George spoke to the couple who had shared their pew, "Guten abend, my name is George Tangeman, and this is my brother, Wilhelm. We are from Sulingen, near Hannover, Prussia."

George and Wilhelm in New York City

"Greetings, we came here from Hamburg fifteen years ago. Fritz and Stella Ringholtz. How long have you been in New York? Do you like it here?" Fritz asked as he shook hands with George.

George replied, "It is a hard life, but better than back home. Here we have jobs. We had hoped to welcome our brother, Carl, to New York, too. He left Prussia with his wife and small children in September. They have not arrived, and now we believe they must be lost at sea."

"I am sorry to hear of your loss. What are your plans now?" Mrs. Ringholtz asked.

Wilhelm was downcast as he recounted they had been in New York for over a year, but now they were leaving for Ohio. "We hope to find land and become farmers in Ohio." He looked away quickly, unable to speak of the loss of Carl and Elizabeth.

"So many German speaking people, mostly Prussians and Bavarians, come to New York and quickly move out west for the opportunity to own land," commented Fritz. "Since we knew the butcher business, we bought a butcher shop on Bowery Street about 10 years ago. Now our two sons run the shop, and we enjoy our grandchildren."

"We have been to Ringholtz Butcher Shop. The liverwurst sausage is very good," smiled George. As the congregation disbursed, Mr. and Mrs. Ringholtz followed George and Wilhelm to the front steps. "It was good to meet you this Christmas Eve. *Frohe Weihnachten*," said George as they parted ways.

"Frohe Weihnachten. Farewell to you both. We wish you a safe journey and much prosperity in Ohio," responded Fritz Ringholtz.

The Tangeman brothers stretched their legs and set a brisk pace back through Kleindeutschland. "You agree? It is time to make our own plans to move west?" asked George.

"The sooner we leave New York, the better off we will be. Carl would want us to find land to farm in the west and start a new life," replied Wilhelm. "We must fulfill his dream to honor his memory."

"Some fellows at work left last month for Ohio. They were looking for land or jobs. I have heard of other German-speaking folks who live there, too," said George.

Wilhelm added, "I heard there was land in Ohio, too, good land for farming. If we leave this winter, do you think we could be in Ohio in time for spring planting?"

"Ja, if we leave right away. It is time to make a fresh start. We have enough money saved for some land, if it is cheap enough, and tools. One of us may need to have a job to pay our other expenses," replied George.

"Do you think our English is good enough to get along?" asked Wilhelm. "I can understand most of what our foreman says."

"Understanding is easier than speaking. We will learn more on the trip out west. I want to go to Ohio this winter. We will be there this spring, tilling and planting," replied George, smiling faintly, turning his mind to their future even though it would be difficult without Carl and his family. Wilhelm took a deep breath and smiled in anticipation of realizing their dream of owning land in America.

The brothers walked the remaining distance to their apartment in somber silence. With the decision to leave New York, they gave up hope of ever seeing Carl again. Silently, the invisible fabric of relationships between George and Wilhelm and the old country had further unraveled. They felt the pain of separation from Carl as they had felt upon leaving Sulingen for America. They each stepped into a season of grief, alone, yet joined in unspoken feelings of loss.

"There is much to be done before we leave for Ohio," stated Wilhelm on Sunday, the day after Christmas. "And we want to work on the dock as much as possible."

"I'll find out about tickets to Ohio this week at the dock," George replied. "Let's go out for a beer to celebrate our plans to move on." He stood up and reached for his oil skin coat. Outside the older, three-story apartment building a dry, fluffy snow was piling up. The brothers began walking up Avenue A, the street for beer halls, theaters, oyster saloons and grocery stores. Noisy exuberance spilled out of biergartens and groups of single people lightheartedly promenaded the avenue. Wilhelm motioned to the Germania, a biergarten for German speakers seeking relaxation and refreshment. They took two steps up four risers into the noisy gathering. At the entrance was a sign advertising a "Sunday Sacred Concert." Inside, patrons socialized with beer and food under the guise of the protection of religious freedom. In this case, the "freedom" was an excuse to circumvent the prevailing "blue laws" forbidding the sale of alcoholic beverages on Sunday. For the German community, Sunday socializing with beer was a deeply held cultural custom from the old country, one they were determined to maintain.

George and Wilhelm joined a table of recent immigrants from the Hannover area. They joined the discussion of a newspaper article of the revolutionary unrest in Prussia in a local German newspaper.

"The German states must unite into one. Prussia, Bavaria, and Austria, too," shouted one man as he raised his fist.

"That will never happen. The local princes are too strong to allow it," replied a short fellow. But change could be felt in the air.

"This newspaper says our home-produced goods like linen and woolen homespun are being replaced by manufactured goods from England. People are losing their incomes to machines," exclaimed another.

"In my village, the only people doing well were the land owners who were producing grain. People always need food," inserted a tall fellow with suspenders over woolen pants. "Everyone else is not doing very well."

The short fellow added, "What we need in Prussia is a better guild system. My father is a blacksmith. At one time he had three apprentices because he had that much business. Now he has not had an apprentice for over a year. With so many people emigrating, there is much less for him to do. And the peasants are much worse off. Some are starving."

"If people are hungry and desperate enough, perhaps a populist movement could succeed...."

Most of the conversation revolved around the old country in a way that reinforced the wisdom of emigrating to America.

Before the brothers left the Germania, Wilhelm bought two bottles of beer in thick, black bottles to enjoy later at home. On the walk home, a steady snow blanketed the streets. Few buggies or wagons were out for pleasure or business on a late Sunday evening. The snow cover added to the mood of cautious well-being in the city between the East and Hudson Rivers.

The following day George inquired at the dock about river and train travel to Ohio. He learned there was a northern route and a southern route. On the northern route, river steamers labored up the Hudson River to Albany throughout the winter. Some tickets were available at a reduced price as cargo passengers. They could work loading and unloading cargo in exchange for part of the cost of their passage.

From Albany passengers and cargo traversed by canal boat on the Erie Canal west to Buffalo, New York, then across Lake Erie by lake steamer to Cleveland, Sandusky or Toledo. Their risk taking the northern route was being caught in ice jams if the temperatures plunged and stayed well below freezing. The southern route was via the Pennsylvania Canal, with inclines up and over the Allegheny Mountains between Philadelphia and Pittsburgh. From Pittsburgh George learned they could travel by river steamer on the Ohio River to the southern part of Ohio. It was a more expensive journey, and George had heard foreboding stories of being lifted in a frightful way over the mountains.

After discussing the two routes with Wilhelm, they decided to save money and purchase the cargo passenger tickets on a river steamer up the Hudson River. From thence, they would travel across New York on the Erie Canal and across Lake Erie to Cleveland. If the winter continued to be mild, they would arrive in Ohio with plenty of time to find land for spring planting in the Cleveland area.

While George returned to the harbor to purchase steamer tickets, Wilhelm prepared their clothing and gear for travel.

First, he cleaned all of their clothing by washing under items and brushing the woolen outerwear. He sewed coins into the hems of their coats as he had watched Mama do when they left Sulingen.

In an hour, George returned with tickets in hand. "We are leaving tomorrow, January 3, 1848. Our steamer, the *Redoubtable*, will depart at 6:00 am."

"We will be ready. I have cleaned our clothing and our coins are secure," announced Wilhelm.

"Danke shöen," replied George. "The trip will be through cold country. We will take all of our extra clothes, our heavy boots, oil cloth coats, food, the medicine kit Mama sent and our Bible, of course."

"Did you buy food for the journey?" asked Wilhelm.

"*Ja*, I bought bread, the dark kind like back home, and meat and cheese from the Ringholtz Market. There is not much fresh produce in the winter, but I found some apples and dried plums," replied George. Wilhelm stacked clothing in the bottom of the carpetbag followed by the medicine kit, Bible and food.

"I suppose it is time to say goodbye to New York. Let's toast to a new life in Ohio with our last bottles of beer," proposed Wilhelm. "Farewell to our first home in America, however humble. It gave us warmth and safety in Kleindeutschland."

"Here's to Kleindeutschland, the shops, the people, a place to socialize and speak German freely," rejoined George.

"And farewell to our harbor jobs. The coldest, wettest work I can imagine. And here's to the coldest, wettest work I can imagine on our own land, raising our own crops, building a good life in Ohio," Wilhelm toasted and laughed heartily.

"Finally, let us toast Carl. To a fine marksman, a good and decent human being, and the best brother in the world. To your family and to you, wherever you are. Surely we will see you in the life to come if you have departed from this one."

On January 3, 1848, the Tangeman brothers left the city of New York from Brooklyn Harbor on the *Redoubtable*, a sturdy, well-traveled river steamer. Land, adventure and the hope for better opportunities drew the brothers forward into their future in the western state of Ohio.

December 26, 1847
Sulingen, Hannover, Prussia

Dear Papa and Mama,

On Christmas Eve we attended the service at Deutsche Evangelische Kirche here in Kleindeutschland in New York. It felt like being in the Sulingen Evangelische Kirche. We sang "O, Tannenbaum" and "Stille Nacht." They sounded much like when we sang in harmony at home, and that made us feel homesick for all of you, especially Carl and family.

It is hopeless to wait for the Yorkshire *to arrive in New York after all this time. The ship is long overdue from a crossing of the Atlantic Ocean. Surely, Carl and Elizabeth have perished to the depths of the ocean. Our hope now is to see them again in the life to come.*

As Carl would wish, we will leave for Ohio in a few days. There are jobs being advertised and other immigrants are moving there to build a better life. Some say there is land we could purchase for an affordable price. We have saved most of our wages and hope to secure land, purchase tools and animals and begin farming this spring. Our next letter will have our new address.

Please pray for our safety and success in this adventure to the western state of Ohio. We think of all of you often and pray for your health and safety in these uncertain times in Prussia.

Your son,
George
New York, New York

Chapter 13
Trip up the Hudson

As winters go, 1848 was a mild one in the city of New York. From their apartment, George and Wilhelm walked to Liverpool dock and took the first ferry across the East River to the Brooklyn Harbor. They boarded the river steamer, *Redoubtable*, at 6:00 am on January 3, 1848. The thermometer read 28 degrees, wind nearly nonexistent, just after low tide. From outside the cabin, they saw and heard the crew cast off and secure the hawsers. Once the *Redoubtable* rounded the tip of Manhattan Island, it made a steady turn north and entered the Hudson River. The city of New York, to the east, had a pink glow in the early morning as the dawn streamed through the buildings of the tenement skyline.

This was the first time the brothers had been more than 20 blocks away from their apartment in Kleindeutschland in the year and a half since they arrived from the old country. They wanted to remember everything they saw; it may be their only trip through the countryside of the state of New York.

The *Redoubtable* glided through the Hudson River at an astounding 18 miles per hour. The speed was made possible by the incoming tide from the Atlantic Ocean. For the next hour, they were being pushed upstream by the rising tide along with the power of the steam engine. To the left a rock formation called the Palisades formed a white ribbon of rock dividing layers of spruce trees on the western shore of the Hudson. Beyond the rocky cliff of Palisades, the river changed.

"Tappen Zee ahead. Named by the Dutch, a river that looks more like the sea," announced Captain Hayes.

"This is some kind of lake," observed Wilhelm. The river channel melted into the broadening expanse of tranquility, as it lost the force of the rising tide. In the crystal stillness, the Hudson River shone like glass. "Look, George, are those geese?" he asked, spotting plump, feathered, ring-necked birds paddling away to the left of the *Redoubtable*.

"If we were closer, I could tell for sure. They look...hey!" George exclaimed as six Canada geese flutter-kicked and wing beat their way clear of the lake surface. Circling in a V-formation, the geese mounted to the heights above and beyond the cliffs of the Palisades. This sighting caused both brothers to be alert and watchful for wildlife as they journeyed north into the wilderness.

"Terrytown on the right. A right pretty inlet. On the northern edge of town is the village of Sleepy Hollow of Washington Irving fame," called Captain Hayes. "This town was established by the Dutch over two centuries before Mr. Irving made it famous in his spooky novel."

"This here lake makes me think of our crossing, but without the waves and sickness. So far, I like this river travel," commented George.

Along the eastern shore, a fishing boat ventured out, three poles over the sides of the boat. At first, all was quiet. Before the *Redoubtable* moved out of sight, the closer fisherman hooked something and began to reel it in. He stood up and the boat began to rock. "It must be a really big fish," observed Wilhelm. As the passengers watched, the fisherman pulled a fish almost as long as he was tall into the boat. The other two helped land the fish and remove the hook. "It must weigh over 60 pounds. What kind of fish is it?" asked Wilhelm.

A short, burly man watching from the bull rail replied, "It may be a sturgeon. That fish is king of the Hudson River."

Captain Hayes asked, "Would you fellas like to trawl for fish for the next hour?" He reduced the speed of the steamer to a slow throb. The crew brought out a trawling net. George and Wilhelm joined half-dozen men willing to let down the net behind the steamer and secure it to the cleats on either side of the aft deck.

An hour later the first mate called out, "Let's haul it up!" The men took their places along the periphery of the trawling net. "One... two... three... pull!" Taking three steps backward, the net came up toward the surface of the Tappen Zee. "Again, one... two... three... pull!" This time the net came partly out of the water, to the groans of the fishermen. "One last time. One... two...three...pull!" Finally, the net was hauled into the boat with enough fish to feed everyone on board for the next few days. Cheers rose from the passengers and crew.

The crew sorted through the fish catch. Smaller ones were thrown back to be caught another time. They were left with two large sturgeons, one striped bass and several smaller herring. Not used to eating fish in the old country or in New York, neither George nor Wilhelm recognized these fish as desirable to eat.

The captain resumed the normal speed of the steamer. At this pace, they could be in Albany, about 150 miles, in two days, but George and William discovered that was not likely. By afternoon, they passed beyond the Tappen Zee and entered the smaller, serpentine river channel of the Hudson River near Stoney Point.

"Lighthouse at Stoney Point on the left. The King's Ferry operated during the American Revolution between Stoney Point and Verplanck on the eastern shore of this river. It was used to ferry soldiers in George Washington's army across the river numerous times to link the northern and southern campaigns," announced Captain Hayes.

"A revolution is a drastic step to take," said Wilhelm, catching the eye of another single fellow traveling alone.

"Ja, the American and the French revolutions had very different outcomes," commented a young man in low tones in his twenties. "My name is Gustav Leitermann. I'm on my way to Ohio."

"So are we," replied George. "I am George Tangeman and this is my brother, Wilhelm." The young men shook hands heartily.

Wilhelm explained, "We want to be in Ohio before spring planting. If we find land near Cleveland, that is where we will settle. We want to farm the land. Do you know anything about farming in America?

"Ja, I know a little. I had a small farm in Pennsylvania. I planted wheat and corn and raised some hogs. Then I broke my leg in an accident with a tree," Gus paused to chuckle. "I could not harvest my crop or take the hogs to market. Instead, I sold them to a neighbor for a lower price. By the time I paid the rent for the land, very little money was left. I sold my hogs and tools to have the money to get to Ohio and buy some land of my own."

"How does renting land work?" asked Wilhelm.

"I planted and harvested for two/thirds of the crop. The owner received one/third as rent. If the crop is good, you can make good money. If not, you better have some animals and a garden to get through the winter," said Gus. "Having a wife helps, too. I haven't been lucky enough to meet someone suitable. I would like to meet someone from the old country. I am from Hamburg, near the Baltic Sea."

"That is not far from our home in Sulingen, near Hannover," continued George. "After we establish our farms, we will want to meet some young ladies from Prussia, too." All three young men shared a chuckle at the thought of finding a group of young women from the old country willing to socialize with the three of them.

Far from the smoke and squalor of New York City, George sat back on the bench along the bull rail on the right side of the bow of the steamer. They had much to learn about the land, the people and how to make a living farming the land in Ohio. Becoming acquainted with Gus was a first step in this physical and mental journey.

"Gus, where do you plan to settle in Ohio? Do you have land in mind already?" asked Wilhelm.

"I have heard of others leaving for Cleveland. The land is dark, thick and rich. I have been told it will grow anything with only a little effort to plough the land, plant the seeds and harvest the crops," answered Gus. "That sounds good to me."

Captain Hayes shouted, "West Point, home of the U.S. Military Academy, up ahead on the left. Cold Spring just beyond on the right. The foundry at Cold Spring supplied artillery during the American Revolution." The stone buildings could barely be seen through spruce trees lining the shore. As the *Redoubtable* came even with the foundry town, a protected cove and dock came into view. On a dead branch towering above the rest, two bald eagles were perched. "American Bald Eagles on the right," pointed Captain Hayes.

As the afternoon unfolded, the engine slowed to navigate the narrow, twisting river channel. Rocky outcrops, stately clumps of spruce and maple trees and tumbling tributaries graced the landscape with unspoiled beauty. At Newburgh, Captain Hayes guided his steamer to the dock on the west side of the Hudson River.

For supper, the cook announced there would be sturgeon steaks, boiled potatoes with butter and bread baked early that morning in the city. After eating their own cooking for a year and a half, George and Wilhelm savored the novel taste of "Albany beefsteak" as sturgeon was known. The passengers sat down to feast on the king of the river, and the cook apologized for not serving the roe of the sturgeon, better known as caviar in Europe. It was simply not the right time of year for this delicacy. The three friends from Prussia could not imagine anything better than what had already been served.

On Tuesday, George, Wilhelm and Gus donned their oil-skin long coats. The day dawned cold and windy with clouds ready to weep. Unlike the scenic day before, the passengers and crew crowded into the long, narrow cabin for shelter. With most passengers indoors, the restricted space quickly became too warm, driving the three friends to the deck seeking shelter out of the wind.

The temperature continued to fall, and Captain Hayes knew the river could freeze solid, stopping their progress to Albany for days or even weeks. By noon the temperature had dipped to 20 degrees. Ice began to form along the shore in between the tributaries. The *Redoubtable* churned against the downstream flow of the river, the only force keeping the ice at bay. The counter movements of the river and steamers kept ice from forming in the center channel. Unlike the previous day, today's speed was about four miles per hour, a slog at best. By dusk, the village of Newburgh came into sight on the left.

"Cargo offload at Newburgh. Move all the parcels on the left side of the deck to the far end of the dock," directed Captain Hayes as he steered the *Redoubtable* close enough to the dock to tie ropes as thick as a snake onto the dockside cleats. George, Wilhelm and Gus lined up with the regular crew to make the cargo transfer. Newburgh was a major crossroads of commerce between Albany and Manhattan and overland via regional turnpikes. In an hour and a half, the goods bound for Newburgh were replaced next to an even greater load for Albany. Past the warehouses at the wharf, the new friends from Prussia followed the main avenue into Newburgh for supper and accommodations. It turned out to be a substantial village with banks, hotels, boardinghouses, churches and impressive homes.

By Wednesday dawn, January 5, the temperature was 12 degrees. The ice along the shore was five inches thicker and extended twice as far across the surface of the river as the previous evening. Captain Hayes cranked up the steamer to a high throb. By 7 am, the *Redoubtable* moved forward and back cracking, crackling and breaking up the icy restraints. Within 30 minutes they were free of the ice, and again moved upstream toward Albany. At that point in time, no one on board believed they would be in Albany before the end of the week or the following week. Unless the thermometer reversed itself soon, the *Redoubtable* would be jammed up, frozen in the Hudson River until spring.

Much to the surprise of passengers and crew alike, by noon of their third day on the Hudson River, the sun came out. Progress up the river was still frustratingly slow, but the ice was no longer thickening and threatening the entire trip. As the mercury in the thermometer rose, so did the spirits of those on the *Redoubtable*.

They emerged from the protective cabin, once again taking in the scenic wonders of plant and animal life and geological features along the river from the main deck.

A woman exclaimed, "What could possibly be on that ice floe? Something is moving."

Captain Hayes replied, "That, my dear lady, is a pair of river seals sunning themselves on this glorious afternoon." The seals raised their heads, as if in greeting, after being introduced by the captain. Ice floes moved downstream at about the same speed of the steamer moving upstream. It required adroit steering to avoid a direct collision. Glancing blows of ice floes a foot thick or more and half the size of the steamer occurred several times that afternoon.

By evening, Captain Hayes announced, "The Village of Poughkeepsie on the right is known for the breweries you see next to the river. This is where we will secure the steamer for the evening. I hope you enjoy the town and the history that lives here," chuckled Captain Hayes. This captain enjoyed informing his passengers of the towns and villages and wild life along the river.

In three more days, the *Redoubtable* achieved the distinction of a relatively quick winter passage to Albany where the Tangeman brothers and most other passengers disembarked. Their last responsibility was discharged with the unloading of 43 boxes and barrels on the Albany Harbor.

The Erie Canal connected with the Hudson River close to the dock where the *Redoubtable* was tied up. The three new friends celebrated the first leg of their journey to Ohio with pub food and a lumpy hotel bed on Erie Canal Way, a street that ran parallel to the famous canal.

Wilhelm was excited to begin the canal portion of their journey to Ohio. He had heard the Erie Canal was the modern "northwest passage," built with only human and animal muscle power and the power of rushing water. German stone masons had done much of the work to create the waterway four feet deep and forty feet wide.

A working boat was due to embark on the return journey to Buffalo and Lake Erie over 400 miles west of Albany. George made inquiries and the three friends signed on as cargo passengers willing to be trained as mule drivers, if needed. They boarded the 14-feet wide, 32-feet long cargo vessel bound for Buffalo, New York on the sunny morning of Sunday, January 9, 1848. The limited size of the canal boat was determined by the size of the 83 locks along the length of the canal.

"Hey, George, look up here," shouted Wilhelm from the top of the cabin of the canal boat. Gus and George climbed the metal ladder to join Wilhelm. From that vantage point they enjoyed the changing scene in a chilly wind as the canal boat was towed through downtown Albany. "That must be the capitol building of the State of New York," added Wilhelm.

George was more interested to see the continuous parade of canal boats on this man-made Northwest Passage of Henry Hudson's fame. He pointed to canal boats laden with grain, lumber, coal and other raw materials moving from the midwestern towns of Cleveland and Toledo, Ohio and Detroit, Michigan toward New York. Gus explained how trade through the Erie Canal and Hudson River made New York the busiest harbor along the eastern seaboard of the United States. Returning the favor, manufactured goods such as textiles, glass and pottery shipped west to supply the growing interior cities and towns.

On this first trip by canal boat, the three friends learned canal boats were powered by teams of horses or mules who walked along a tow path. Along the north edge of the Erie Canal a tow path had been beaten smooth by the hooves of hundreds of mules and horses moving both east and west since the opening of the canal in 1825. With cargo and passenger boats traversing both directions simultaneously, George was curious to learn what system allowed the boats to keep moving.

The canal boat near the tow path (north) side of the canal had the right of way. At the same time the other boat kept to the berm (south) side of the canal. The driver of the team of horses or mules, the hoggee, of the priority boat kept his team nearer to the canal side of the tow path at the same time the driver of the lower priority team stopped at the far side of the tow path and created slack in the tow line from his team. The priority boat's team stepped over the slack line while the priority boat was pulled over the sunken tow line. When the priority boat was clear, the other team would retrieve its tow line and continue on its way. Wilhelm was impressed with how smoothly this complex process occurred dozens of times a day.

When a six hour shift of a team of mules ended, the canal boat stopped to swap the fresh team on board the canal boat for the exhausted animals on shore. From the stable on board at the stern of the boat, the animals were housed and cared for along the length of the canal.

On January 12, midway between Fort Plain and Herkimer, New York, Gus, George and Wilhelm were called upon to assist to bring a tired team of mules back onto the canal boat.

"Hey, krauts, give us a hand with these stubborn mules. We can't be on our way until these stupid mules are back on board," called the captain of the canal boat. The three friends joined four other crew members determined to reverse the stubbornness into cooperation with sheer force. One fellow shouted and slapped his hand on the rump of the recalcitrant mule while the others pulled forward. This made the mule dig in his hooves even harder.

"OK, time to bring out the block and tackle," sighed a tall, broad-shouldered Swede. "Connect this strap to the harness," he directed Gus. "Now men, you two push, while you two pull on this lever." With the pulley contraption, they were finally able to apply enough force to get the stubborn mule to take a step forward onto the ramp into the stable area. Once he took one step, the stubbornness snapped, yielding to the pull of the block and tackle and the allure of food and water on board. The second mule nearly scampered after the first.

The Tangemans' journey on the Erie Canal unfolded through shift changes of mule teams and passage through locks designed to lift the canal boats from the level of the Hudson River to Lake Erie. In Syracuse, New York, their canal boat was scheduled to be weighed to calculate the toll charge.

Gus asked the Swede how the canal boat would be weighed. "At the beginning of the season each canal boat was weighed empty. Our canal boat will enter the weigh lock. Then they drain away the canal, and the boat comes to rest on the scale. The toll is calculated based on what is being transported and how much it weighs. Judging by the canal traffic this winter, a lot of trade comes to the cities along the Erie Canal.

George was interested to learn the city of Rochester, New York benefitted directly from the opening of the Erie Canal. A brisk trade in grain flowing through on canal boats, propelled Rochester to become the milling center for wheat in the northeast in the 1830s and 1840s. George mused that the wheat he and Wilhelm raised would find a ready market in Rochester. Other cities along the canal attracted industries and population to produce goods such as textiles, glass and pottery.

In Buffalo, goods from the Erie Canal were offloaded into warehouses or directly onto lake steamships. The Buffalo Harbor was teaming with people, most of them seeking passage west to Ohio and beyond. There was plenty of work available loading and offloading goods.

By January 24, the weather turned bitter cold. It began to snow on the Monday they were trying to leave for Cleveland. The visibility was only six feet, declared by the harbormaster insufficient to safely traverse Lake Erie. They stayed three more days until the storm passed. On January 27 they boarded the *Buffalo Belle*, a combination passenger and cargo vessel bound for Cleveland.

George and Wilhelm were in high spirits as they approached Cleveland on January 28.

"I couldn't help overhearing you are going to Cleveland to begin farming," interjected a fellow traveler, Jakob Frankheimer. "I rented a farm near Ashland, Ohio for three years. I lost everything I had put into the place when the price of wheat dropped like a stone. All the good land is gone. When an acreage is available, the price is more than $3.50 an acre. Ja, the farming can be good, but it is too expensive around Cleveland."

"But we heard the price of land was less than $2.00 per acre," replied Wilhelm. "At those prices, we cannot afford to buy land here in Cleveland."

In low tones, George said to Wilhelm, "Let's try our own luck with the land. We might find something affordable."

The three friends left the *Buffalo Belle* and headed toward the central commercial district of Cleveland. George visited a bank, Wilhelm a tavern and Gus a livery stable. By late afternoon, they rendezvoused for supper.

"That fellow, Jakob, was right. According to the bank, it is hard to find any land less than $3.60 per acre. The demand for land is high from new immigrants and all of the early parcels have been claimed years ago," related George.

Gus and Wilhelm heard similar accounts of the prices of land in northeast Ohio. "We could move across the state by land, or we could find another steamer and go further west in Ohio. I heard there is still land being sold by the government in the Toledo area," responded Gus.

"Let's find another steamer. It is faster and easier to cover a long distance," suggested Wilhelm. The friends stayed overnight in Cleveland, boarded a steamer toward Toledo, and arrived on February 1. Much to their disappointment, Toledo was situated next to the Great Black Swamp. The land for sale was situated in these lowlands. Unscrupulous land swindlers sometimes sold untillable parcels to unsuspecting immigrants who responded to newspaper ads from afar.

Finding no land with which to begin their farming ventures, George, Wilhelm and Gus were discouraged. They chose to find work on the Harbor of Toledo while they decided their next step. Gus decided he would go back to Cleveland. The livery stable he visited was hiring and he knew horses. After an evening together, the friends parted amicably the next morning.

The Tangeman brothers considered their options. They could take the Miami and Erie Canal south to Cincinnati, travel overland across Ohio, return the way they had come from Cleveland, continue to another Lake Erie city or stay in Toledo. George and Wilhelm bought passage on a canal boat to Cincinnati on February 6. They'd heard there might be land available at lower prices further away from Lake Erie. If not, there were bound to be good jobs in the meat packing industry in Cincinnati. With a resigned determination, the brothers departed Toledo on a canal boat headed south.

"Carl would like to be here, getting ready to start farming this spring," said George.

"Ja, I still can't believe he is really gone," replied Wilhelm wistfully.

Chapter 14
Carl in New York City

Carl arrived in New York City on a wind-whipped Sunday afternoon, January 23, 1848. The slow steamer from Philadelphia labored to weave through ice chunks, the bow screaming as it scraped against the icy impediments. There was no escape from the ear-rasping torture of iron hull smashing chunks of floating ice.

When the skyline of New York came into sight, Carl felt both exhilarated at the prospect of seeing his brothers and bone weary from his cross-country journey. The guiding goal of his life since he left Sulingen, survived the storm at sea and withstood the deaths of Elizabeth and his children in New Orleans had been to achieve this moment—arriving in New York. He felt certain he could find people in Kleindeutschland who knew Wilhelm and George and they would lead him to their reunion quickly.

As his foot landed on the wooden pier, frigid knife winds sliced at his oil-skin coat. Thoughts of his brothers swirled as he pulled his cap around his ears, bent forward following the crowd down the pier, up the steps and on to South Street.

Hearing German being spoken on his right, Carl paused to ask directions to Kleindeutschland. "You cannot miss it. Go past South Street and Front Street to Water Street. Follow Water to your right until you smell the best 'kraut 'n' brats in America. Turn left a few blocks and you are there—Kleindeutschland." Carl followed the direction pointed, soon surrounded by sounds of his native tongue, some more like his own Prussian dialect, others from Saxony or Bavaria. Even in his exhaustion, he looked for familiarity in every face. Could this one or that one be George or Wilhelm?

Mud and manure were everywhere clogging up the streets, slowing down traffic. The icy rain turned dirt to mud under the clopping hooves of horses on Water Street. The street was crowded with wagons and carriages transporting people and cargo. Carl tried to stay on the wooden sidewalks to avoid slipping in the mud and being trampled by a team of draft horses.

As dark settled in, the crowd began to thin. Carl gave up his search for this day and vowed to begin in the morning. Hoping for a sense of home like he had found in Cincinnati, Carl stopped at three boardinghouses before he found the Berlin House serving supper of sauerbraten and dumplings and the sleep he craved.

His hopes rose in the morning with the crystalline sun. Temperatures had fallen below zero degrees over night, enough to keep all but the most hardy New Yorkers indoors. Undaunted, Carl began his search for places described in his brothers' letters; the harbor, the social clubs that sponsored marksman competitions and biergartens.

His hopes were high as he approached the harbor. Surely, George and Wilhelm would be working on a Monday. He patrolled up and down the pier, hoping to find one of them and rejoice in their surprise and joy. "Bitte, do you know my brothers, George and Wilhelm Tangeman?" he asked of a foreman who paused between orders as he barked at his dockworkers. The first two ignored him. The third spit out, "I don't know any names of my dockworkers," and turned his back. Carl spent the day walking slowly up and down the pier looking for his brothers. At the end of the day, he was exhausted and feeling discouraged. He had been so certain he could find George and Wilhelm where they worked. He could only imagine they had found jobs elsewhere, away from the strenuous, dirty work on the docks.

On his way back to the Berliner Boardinghouse, Carl bought a copy of the New Yorker *Staats-Zeitung*, a daily newspaper in German. He was anxious for news from his homeland. Most of the newspaper was filled with local happenings such as German dances, competitions and social events. Weddings among the leading German families received full press coverage. Interspersed among these was the news of mounting revolutionary unrest in Europe. Food shortages continued and military skirmishes had broken out in local areas of Prussia. Revolutionary war could break out at any time in France, Italy, Prussia, Austria or Ireland.

Exhausted from a day of walking and looking for Wilhelm and George, Carl fell into bed determined to find out something about his brothers the next day.

At breakfast the next morning, Carl asked his fellow boarder, Mr. Grohle, "I need to search for my brothers in Kleindeutsch-land. Where would you suggest I start?"

"Kleindeutschland is between Bowery and Avenue D, on the lower East Side. You will find many biergartens, sport clubs, schools, apartments and churches. If you check at the post office, you may discover whether you brothers have been in to check their mail recently. Good luck in your search."

"Where might I find the post office?" asked Carl.

"It has been operating in the Middle Dutch Church on Nassau Street for over a dozen years. You will find it about a half dozen blocks west of the docks," replied Mr. Grohle.

After breakfast, Carl began to methodically walk every street in Kleindeutschland. On Avenue D, he stopped at every establishment that was open for business. He stopped at every factory and small workshop in the neighborhood as places where groups of German speaking individuals gathered. His eyes furtively searched every face for a mutual recognition.

Carl began his search with high hopes. He inquired diligently as he walked the entire length of Avenue D in Kleindeutschland. He could tell where the German area began and ended by the smells of roasted sausages and the languages heard in the street. At the end of the day he again walked the docks in search of George and Wilhelm or someone who knew them. On his way back to his boardinghouse, Carl strode Nassau Street to the Post Office in the Middle Dutch Church. In the decrepit 200-year-old building, Carl inquired, "I'm here to collect any pieces of mail for the name of Tangeman."

In a few minutes, the clerk returned, "Sorry."

On the fifth day, Carl walked the length of Bowery Street, and tried, with difficulty, to maintain hope he could find his brothers. Even so, he persisted in his search of Kleindeutschland, knocking on every door, entering every establishment. Two people at a shooting club thought they may have met Wilhelm and George, but they were not sure.

On the way home Carl stopped at the post office. Again, he asked if there were any letters for "Tangeman." In a few minutes the clerk returned with one letter.

"Danke," returned Carl.

Back out on the street, Carl eagerly opened the letter addressed to George from their father, Friedrich Tangemann in Sulingen.

On Saturday, January 29, 1848, Carl's sixth day in New York City, he searched the cross streets of Kleindeutschland. With each step he came closer to the reality that he may not find Wilhelm and George in New York.

LETTER FROM FRIEDRICH TANGEMAN IN
SULINGEN, HANNOVER, PRUSSIA TO GEORGE AND
WILHELM TANGEMAN IN NEW YORK

December 11, 1847
New York, New York

Dear George and Wilhelm,
   I am writing to you with sad news from Carl. His ship, the Yorkshire, *blew off course and finally arrived in New Orleans. While there,*

Elizabeth, Dorothee and wee David perished to a fever. Carl survived and is on his way to find you in New York. He will need your support and help to survive this loss.

The price of food is still high, and there was a protest riot in Berlin. Too many people are hungry, and there is unrest everywhere. We are as well as can be. The rumors of war are good for the saddlery business. We have many orders for saddles for the cavalry. Uncle Gottlob suffered an injury to his left hand in his woodworking shop, but he is healing now.

We miss you, but we know you are doing well in America. I pray you reunite with Carl soon.

Your father,
F.T. (Friedrich Tangemann)
Sulingen, Hannover, Prussia

Sunday, January 30, dawned clear and mild. Carl was profoundly discouraged. The goal of finding George and Wilhelm that had urged him across country from New Orleans to New York now seemed beyond his grasp. He felt alone and lonely. He would need to rebuild his life by himself, all the while exhausted and weary from his quest. Without George and Wilhelm he could not envision a path forward.

As Carl stepped onto the street, he decided to seek comfort in attending a church service, like the one where he had been baptized and married in Sulingen. The language, the people, the music and the cultural values drew him toward the Deutsch Evangelische Reformiert Kirche at the corner of Montgomery and Madison Streets. Carl walked slowly allowing the enormity of his predicament to penetrate his consciousness.

An unseasonably warm day brought many parishioners to the service. As Carl approached the crowd that had gathered on the front steps, he decided to do something uncharacteristic for himself. This was a last desperate plea for help from a man used to knowing what to do, and leading others. He walked up to the growing gathering of worshippers and proclaimed in a loud voice, "My name is Carl Tangeman. I am from Sulingen, near

Hannover, Prussia. Bitte, do you know my brothers George and Wilhelm Tangeman? Have any of you ever met George or Wilhelm Tangeman here in New York?"

At first the crowd hushed to quiet, embarrassed by this display of raw emotion. Carl looked across the faces for any sign of recognition. Heads shook and eyes cast down with murmurs of "Bitte, bitte."

Carl's head slumped, tears starting to form in the corners of his eyes. Slowly moving from the edge of the crowd, an older couple made their way through the crowd to greet Carl. "Guten morgan. My name is Fritz Ringholtz and this is my wife, Stella. We met your brothers on Christmas Eve. They attended the church service in this church. We visited with them after the service. They told us they had been waiting for you to arrive by ship, but had given up hope of ever seeing you again."

Carl was stunned. These were the first people he met who had actually known his brothers in New York. "What else did they say? Do you know where I could find them?"

Stella joined the conversation, "They were so sad they lost you and your family."

"Do you know where they are? How can I get in touch with them?" pleaded Carl.

Fritz replied, "I am so sorry, Carl. Your brothers told us they had plans to leave for Ohio."

Carl was caught up in a confusion of emotions. At last, he found someone who knew his brothers in New York. Again he had reason to hope he could find them. But, Ohio was an enormous state. It may be impossible. Or they may change their plans and go elsewhere in this vast new country. At least he had a direction, and a new possibility to find his brothers.

"Danke, danke schöen!" Carl exclaimed. "This is good news. Now I will go to Ohio. I may still find my brothers!" He reached out and shook hands with Fritz and Stella, tears glistening in his eyes. Carl had come so close to giving up hope and closing the chapter of his brothers in his life. He knew caution was more prudent than optimism. At the same time, now he had reason to believe he could find his brothers if they were still in Ohio. For the moment, he only felt relief and optimism.

"Will you come to our home for dinner?" asked Stella. "We would like to hear your story of coming to this country."

"Ja, ja," replied Carl. "Do you mean now? I will be leaving for Ohio tomorrow."

"Ja, now. Come with us after the service, and we will have Sunday dinner together," assured Fritz.

Carl enjoyed the liverwurst, bratwurst sausages, warm potatoes with onions and apples. It was the best meal he had eaten in a very long time, partly for the familiar food and partly for the company of Fritz and Stella Ringholtz. During the afternoon Carl related how his ship was blown off course, Elizabeth and the children died in New Orleans, Carl himself almost lost his life in the steamboat collision on the Mississippi River, traveling up the Ohio River, making friends in Cincinnati and coming up and over the Allegheny Mountains in Pennsylvania. Carl's friendship with the Ringholtz' deepened as he shared the feelings of his heart about the hardships he had endured and his renewed hope of finding his brothers.

On Monday, January 31, 1848, Carl packed his few belongings and returned to the Brooklyn Harbor on the 7:00 am ferry across the East River. He walked the dock until he located a steamship departing later that day for Philadelphia. While he waited, Carl purchased a German language newspaper, the *New Yorker Staats-Zeitung*, the premier newspaper with news by and for German readers. He settled back, watched the frigate birds and breathed in the salty breeze. The front page story was about continued tensions in Prussia fed by poor crops and the potato blight spreading across central Europe. The industrial bourgeoisie was frustrated by limitations on industrial expansion which allowed England to continue to lead the industrial revolution. Their goods were lower in price. Commerce in Prussia has been depressed which meant lower incomes and lower demand for food and goods. Carl realized the difficult situation he had left in Prussia had become even worse.

By late morning, the *Fletcher* pulled away from the dock loaded with cargo and passengers. Entering the East River, a stiff wind blew out of the north propelling the packet ship southward shortening the time to Philadelphia. On Wednesday afternoon, February 2, Carl stepped off the *Fletcher* at the docks in Philadelphia. As with most return trips, it seemed shorter, more direct, less time consuming than the outward trip from Philly to New York had been. Due to a minor repair to the pulley mechanism, the Pennsylvania Canal and Allegheny Portage Railroad canal boat was delayed until Friday morning, February 4.

Knowing the harrowing experience of his initial trip through Pennsylvania, Carl entered this canal boat on a railroad train car with realistic trepidation. The first leg of this journey began on a morning as crisp, clear and cold as water gushing from a mountain spring. Carl hardly noticed his surroundings, and he hardly felt the morning. His mind was on his new search for Wilhelm and George in Ohio.

Having a friend in Cincinnati drew him in that direction. He thought of her work with the Underground Railroad and believed he could be of service to that cause. He could also help her at the boardinghouse, and perhaps she would have an idea of how to start his search.

In reverse of his initial trip across Pennsylvania, the canal boat was transferred from the train car at Columbia and Carl continued this leg of the trip by canal boat to Holidaysburg. The first of five upward inclines loomed overhead. As the stationary steam engine bellowed smoke, the wheels and steel cables screeched into service. Slowly, the first incline was mounted at a steep angle reminiscent of the angle of a mast in an ocean storm.

Carl's second trip across Pennsylvania was uneventful, much like the first. He kept to himself in an attempt not to arouse negative comments about his German language and immigrant status. There were a few others he heard speaking German in low tones, but he chose not to join those conversations either.

These canal boat passengers spent three nights in the same accommodations as Carl's first trip over the mountains. Arriving in Pittsburgh on February 7, 1848, Carl felt relief when the canal boat was pulled over the aqueduct to the 2nd Avenue basin.

Compared with his initial discovery of Pittsburgh, this visit was damp, gray and grim in a winter that seemed to be stalled on its progression toward spring. It was neither cold enough to freeze nor warm enough to prepare for planting spring crops. In homes and taverns, churches and boardinghouses, if a person moved more than a few feet away from the direct heat of stove or hearth, his or her body wavered between shiver and shake. The stabbing cold reminded Carl of winter in Sulingen without the benefit of several family members to keep a small house warm.

Carl was anxious to continue his journey to Cincinnati as soon as possible. Without even stopping at Mrs. Bittleman's boarding house, Carl walked directly to the point of the tributaries of the Ohio River where the City of Pittsburgh was situated. Returning to the new docks on the Monongahela River, he was told few river vessels had left Pittsburgh in the past three days. The fog at river's edge was thick, murky and raw. Even so, he found one river steamer preparing to depart. He hailed the captain to ask about passage to Cincinnati, and Captain Jack Rawlins shouted back, "Load in those barrels and boxes, now! It's time to cast off." He motioned for Carl to join three muscled crew members as they shuffled quickly toward the dock side of the river steamer.

The four men grunted and hoisted barrels of glass bowls, drinking glasses and wine goblets packed in sawdust onto the *Three Sisters*. Simultaneously, the boiler came to life, its clatter and throb spreading like a Tin Pan Alley band serenading the City of Pittsburgh, the Allegheny, Monongahela and Ohio Rivers. Carl breathed a prayer of thanks for this captain who had just hired him and would provide his passage to Cincinnati.

January 30, 1848
Sulingen, Hannover, Prussia

Dear Papa and Mama,

I arrived in New York a week ago. I have looked for George and Wilhelm in the Kleindeutschland of New York. I walked on every street and stopped at every shop, biergarten, social hall and church. No one knew George and Wilhelm. Finally, I found a couple, Mr. and Mrs. Ringholtz, at the Deutsch Evangelische Reformiert Kirche. They met my brothers on Christmas Eve at the church. They told the Ringholtz' they had given up hope of ever finding me. They decided to go to Ohio to become farmers. Tomorrow I will leave for Ohio to look for them again.

Your letter arrived at the New York Post Office this week. I realize my brothers do not know I am alive and looking for them.

New York is a city of many, many people in small apartments. In Kleindeutschland there are artisan shops, such as bakeries, locksmiths and cabinet makers. Many buildings have a workshop in the basement, a store on the street level and a market for selling fruits and vegetables under an awning in front. The upper levels are small apartments. One or two families live in each apartment. They have barely enough space for everyone to sleep on the floor. I understand why George and Wilhelm wanted to move west to start a better life.

I have thought about coming back to Sulingen to begin again. But, there is nothing for me there. Only war and starvation. Elizabeth and the children are gone. My old life is gone with them. My only path is to move toward Ohio to once again try to find George and Wilhelm the way God has laid out for me.

You and my sisters are always in my prayers.

Your son,
Carl
New York, New York

Shrouded in fog, the *Three Sisters* slowly prevailed down the Ohio River, mile by mile. The captain of this river steamer would realize triple his usual profits if he could deliver the glass goods downstream to Cincinnati by February 15. He was willing to take the risk of traveling in the river fog, risk to his own life, his steamer, the glassware, crew and passengers. He believed the noisy steam engine served as sufficient warning to the few flatboats, steamers, packets or showboats moving up or down the Ohio River in the dead of winter. Most captains of vessels chose not to venture on the river until the fog lifted and the sun revealed villages, forests, fields, snags and other river craft. Captain Rawlins, a contrarian, had made a small fortune delivering goods at times and to places shunned by others. This trip may be his last, if it yielded enough profit to secure his retirement.

In the persistent fog the *Three Sisters* seemed to make slower progress than if they were advancing through black strap molasses. Their only stops were to drop anchor for the night and to take on wood and coal to keep the boiler fired up during the daytimes: Steubenville, Ohio to Newport, Ohio to Williamstown, Virginia to Parkersburg, Virginia.

Arriving at dusk on the evening of February 11, at the docks of Parkersburg, the fog abruptly lifted. Carl realized he had been deeply worried the past four days, reliving the collision between the *Talisman* and *Tempest* steam boats on the Mississippi River that nearly took his life. He was relieved to move beyond the fog-bound portion of the trip on the Ohio River. For the first time since he left New York, Carl slept deeply and woke up feeling refreshed.

At first light Captain Rawlins throttled up his aging steamboat, steered to the left toward the main channel and surged downstream. The obstacles in the river and competing traffic were visible now, but it seemed to make little difference to the captain of the *Three Sisters*. Drawing closer to Cincinnati, the crew arose early and stoked the boiler. Throughout the day they took turns at the bow of the steamer, watching for snags and sandbars in the river.

Pomeroy, Ohio; Glenwood, Kentucky; Ironton, Ohio; Stout, Ohio. As Carl passed each of these towns and cities and others in Ohio, he wondered if George and Wilhelm may have already arrived and settled into a community in Ohio. Fields and farms, especially, led him to think his brothers could be close by. He imagined the routes they may have followed and dreamed of finding them in Ohio at last.

By the night before the February 15 deadline, both captain and crew of the *Three Sisters* were exhausted. In the past seven days, Carl worked harder than he had on any other steamers moving on the Mississippi or Ohio Rivers. He endured both danger and tedium to attain his goal of returning to the one city familiar to him in Ohio. Even without the promise of triple wages, Carl would have been willing to work this much and more, as well as endure the risky journey in the fog, to return to Cincinnati, Ohio so quickly.

Chapter 15
Found

George and Wilhelm Tangeman left Toledo, Ohio on February 6, 1848, traveling south by canal boat on the Miami and Erie Canal. The teams of horses and mules towed the brothers in a smooth, swift trip southward from Toledo, Ohio. They arrived at the canal station in Cincinnati as the sun disappeared behind low western hills on February 9. They gladly left their "boat legs" in favor of the firm earth. River, canal and lake travel were only an expedited conveyance on their way to a future in farming.

"That Scottish fellow on the canal boat said there might be land for sale west of Cincinnati," said Wilhelm while he hefted his carpet bag onto his shoulder. "He said to head out west from the canal boat station." The brothers followed the sunlight away from the center of the city on foot. The buildings thinned out in less than a mile, and they began to see open areas, not yet being tilled. On the left side of the street, next to a livery stable, the Ohio Boarding House caught their attention. It was dusk, and they were weary from the constant motion during their weeks on water.

After breakfast, George and Wilhelm walked next door and engaged horses at the Lichty Livery Stable. They rode west along Cleve's Pike in search of reasonably priced land. Within a mile they stopped at a farm with white frame house, large post-and-beam barn and low hog shed.

"Sprechen sie Deutsch?" asked Wilhelm as he approached the farmer feeding dairy cattle next to a wooden barn.

"Ja, ja. My name is Jacob Doering, and I am from Oldenburg, three years ago now," replied the round-faced farmer, blue eyes peeking out from a thick brown beard and moustache.

"My name is Wilhelm Tangeman and this is my brother, George," continued Wilhelm. "We just arrived in Cincinnati from New York. We are looking to buy farm land."

"Ach, you should have come when we did. Now there are so many newcomers from the old country. Everyone wants land," commented the farmer. "There is not so much left."

"Is there any land for sale in this area?" asked George.

"Let me see…. I think I heard of some land down that road, and then turn right for about a mile or so on the right," was the answer. "Many trees still need to be cleared to make way for the plough."

"Danke, we appreciate your help," replied Wilhelm. "Auf Wiedersehen."

By noon George and Wilhelm located the land that still needed to be cleared of a scattering of oaks, maples and syca-mores along with willow brush growing wild. They understood why this parcel had not been purchased. It was small, perhaps not more than eight to ten acres. A creek ran through the middle with steep banks and gullies carved out exposing a rocky outcrop of sandstone. After clearing the land, the owner could expect to have only four or five acres of tillable soil. It was not enough acreage to seriously consider for purchase.

In the following days, George and Wilhelm rented horses and rode through most of the outlying areas of Hamilton County surrounding Cincinnati. They also spent time at biergartens and social clubs in Over-the-Rhine. There they met other German speaking immigrants and inquired about how to find land and get a start in farming. They learned that most of the farm land in Hamilton County had already been purchased and was being farmed. Only a few areas of the county were yet to be sold by the government, mostly school sections from a few townships. They were told a school section was a square mile that had been set aside within a township of 36-square miles for the establishment of a school. Announcements of upcoming school section sales could be found in local newspapers.

On February 15, Captain Rawlins was jubilant to see the smoke-belching saw mills at the edge of Cincinnati. It was the largest inland city of the United States at that time, a smoky, dirty and rich city thriving on the trade of agricultural products and pork bellies going downstream to feed the burgeoning slave trade and cotton plantations in the South.

The *Three Sisters* reached the wharf of Cincinnati near dusk. Quickly and carefully, the crew loaded the expensive shipment of glass goods into a wharf side warehouse. Finally, with wages in hand, Carl walked quickly up from "the Bottoms" toward Broadway. This time he kept a keen eye for trouble from local dockworkers and laborers. He kept to himself and encountered no difficulties. In about forty minutes, Carl knocked on the door of Mrs. Stolz' boardinghouse. Step falls of sturdy shoes approached and the door swung open.

"Carl!" exclaimed Mrs. Stolz. "What a surprise to see you back in Cincinnati. Come in, come in."

Carl looked into the blue-gray eyes of his best friend in America, and felt like he had come home. "Ja, it is good to be back in Cincinnati. I hope you have a room for me?" Carl inquired as he grasped Mrs. Stolz' outstretched hands with both of his.

"Of course, your old room is ready for you," Mrs. Stolz said as she looked at Carl, checking for injuries. "How are you? Have you had supper?"

Carl replied, "I am in good health. No encounters with the local English this time," he chuckled. "And, no I have not had any supper. Is that borscht I smell?"

"Ja, I will serve you in the dining room. The others finished a short while ago," Mrs. Stolz said. Mrs. Stolz' thick beet soup with dark bread still tasted much like the soup his mother made in Sulingen. When Carl finished, he delivered his belongings upstairs to his room.

Hearing Carl's boots coming down the front stairway, Mrs. Stolz smiled broadly. She led Carl to the front parlor and introduced him to three other boarders.

"Will you join us for a cup of coffee, Carl?" asked Mrs. Stolz.

"Yes, I enjoy your coffee very much," returned Carl as he relaxed in the parlor.

"Would you like to share your recent adventures with all of us?" urged Mrs. Stolz, eager to hear the account of Carl's travels that brought him back to Cincinnati.

"Ja, that would be fine. Perhaps I will provide your evening's entertainment," Carl replied with a twinkle in his eye.

Carl told about his initial trip up the Ohio River to Pittsburgh. He was careful not to mention the *Convoy* steamer being part of the Underground Railroad. His other stories of the utopia town and bounty hunters were met with interest. His listeners chimed in with their own accounts of river adventures, too. When Carl's travel account reached Pittsburgh, Carl explained how he chose the quickest route to New York, the Pennsylvania Canal and Allegheny Portage Railroad.

Mrs. Stolz had heard of the canal, incline and railroad to Philadelphia, but she had never known anyone who actually made the dreadful trip. Carl described in some detail how the incline allowed a steam engine to pull a steel cable attached to a canal boat up the mountain. Traversing five inclines on each side of the mountains, passengers traveled from Pittsburgh to Philadelphia in merely four days. From Philadelphia, Carl related how he reluctantly booked passage on another steamer and finally arrived in New York.

After an exhaustive search of Kleindeutschland in New York, Carl explained how he had all but given up ever seeing George and Wilhelm. In desperation, he shouted his name and asked for help from the congregation at the Evangelische Kirche. Excitedly, he described meeting Stella and Fritz Ringholtz and how they invited him to their home. George and Wilhelm had also met the Ringholtz couple on Christmas Eve, a few days before they left New York City. They confided they had given up on Carl and left to start new lives farming in Ohio. With this encouraging information Carl was back in Cincinnati to begin a new search for his brothers in Ohio.

Mrs. Stolz listened intently to Carl's story. Ohio was a large state with many thousands of people, but she did not want to discourage her friend in his quest. She only said, "How can I help you find your brothers?"

"I need a place to stay, while I decide how to proceed. Tomorrow is soon enough to begin my search," Carl responded with a smile that brought smiles and chuckles from his audience.

Mr. Kritchner offered, "You are fortunate to know your brothers are in Ohio. If you desire, I will ask the other German speakers at the sawmill if they have heard of your Tangeman brothers."

Mr. Lutz, a school teacher for a local German elementary school explained, "There are several churches in Over-the-Rhine where many German speaking people gather. I could ask the church leaders to make announcements in their churches or church newspapers."

Finally, Mr. Eck offered, "I belong to the Frankfurter Social Club. If you like, I will make inquiries and post a notice on the bulletin board in the front hallway. From time to time, other German speakers come there to try to find family or friends," offered Mr. Eck.

Carl beamed with gratitude for these offers of help. Like a pebble tossed into a pond, Carl hoped these offers of help would create ever widening circles of inquiry that eventually would lead him to reunion with George and Wilhelm.

On February 16, 1848 Carl began a personal search for his brothers in the Over-the-Rhine neighborhood of Cincinnati, an area about half the size of Kleindeutschland in New York. Again, Carl set out to systematically knock on every door and ask anyone who would listen about his brothers. He also sought out places to leave a written message for George and Wilhelm or anyone who may know them.

By Wednesday, February 23, Carl had approached every German-speaking person he met in Over-the-Rhine with no recognition of their family name.

That evening at supper Carl announced to Mrs. Stolz and his new friends, "I have been here a week knocking on every door in Over-the-Rhine. It is time for me to get a job to support myself." Although Carl had saved part of his wages from working on the *Three Sisters*, he needed a job to support his search for his brothers. It could be a very long time before they were found, if the search could be successful.

"There are always jobs available at the meat packing plants," suggested Mr. Eck. "It is hard work, but the money is decent, until you find something you like better."

"Mr. Tangeman," called Mr. Kritchner from the far end of the table. "I am sorry to report no one has met or heard of your brothers at the sawmill. I will ask new employees, and post a message on the message board about your inquiry."

"Danke, danke," replied Carl. "I appreciate you spreading the word about George and Wilhelm. Someone may know something eventually. And today I posted a message in the *Christliche Apologete German Methodist* newspaper. There's a section for German speaking persons to find family members and friends."

Mr. Lutz related news from the old country he had read in another German language newspaper. Prussia, Austria, Italy and France had launched their 1848 year of revolution. He read that change was needed to reform antiquated political structures and spur industrial progress. A lively discussion ensued as each person from a German-speaking state shared his perspective about the news of looming revolutions and their thoughts about German unification.

On Thursday, February 24, George bounded up the steps into their boardinghouse after work waving a copy of a German newspaper. "Wilhelm, the school section of Green Township in Hamilton County has been placed for sale to the public. That is 640 acres new to the market." George was excited at the prospect of such a large parcel of land being sold at auction. It was scheduled for Monday, February 28.

Wilhelm smiled for the first time in Cincinnati, "Let's go look at that section on Sunday. I'll arrange to hire horses from the Lichty Livery."

At breakfast on Sunday, February 27, 1848, Wilhelm turned to his fellow boarders and asked, "George and I may attend a land auction tomorrow. Do any of you know how such an auction is conducted here in Cincinnati?"

A lively discussion of auctions of various sorts ensued. An auctioneer led the bidding and continued until only one bid was on the table after the other bidders dropped out. That person won the bid and bought the item being sold. One man had been to livestock auctions including thoroughbred horses. Others had seen household goods, tools and livery goods sold in this manner. "It is an exciting way to purchase property, and sometimes you can buy at a low price."

While Wilhelm and the other boarders shared stories, George picked up the newspaper to check the time and place for the auction. It was scheduled for 10:00 am, Monday, February 28 at the Hamilton County Court House. He glanced over the rest of the newspaper, and for the first time an announcement on the last page leaped from the page:

'If you know George or Wilhelm Tangeman from Sulingen, Hannover, Prussia, please contact Carl Tangeman at Mrs. Stolz' boardinghouse on Walnut Street in Over-the-Rhine."

Years later, Wilhelm recalled the crisp crunch of snow crushing under pounding boots and George often remembered that moment when he smelled a horse's sweat.

For George, the emergency of the possibility that Carl might be alive was nerve shattering. He could hardly breathe or move or think until this possibility was confirmed or dashed in disappointment. Immediately, George and Wilhelm grabbed coats, ducked under the front stoop, leaped off the front porch and ran to Lichty Livery next door. They offered to saddle the horses themselves, as they grabbed bridles, blankets and saddles. Breathlessly, both brothers mounted and spurred the drowsy gelding and mare to an immediate gallop. The horses' hooves crushed ice particles freshly frozen overnight. Riding at breakneck speed from Cleve's Pike east to downtown Cincinnati, the riders arrived at Over-the-Rhine along Liberty Street in less than 10 minutes. Slowing enough to make the turn left on Walnut Street, they cantered up the street watching for the sign for Mrs. Stolz' Boardinghouse.

"There it is," shouted George, pointing to the two-story white frame house on the right and the sign above the front door, Mrs. Stolz' Boardinghouse. In one continuous motion, both brothers turned their horses toward the front porch, crashed to the ground, secured their horses' reins to the porch railing and took the three steps up the front porch in a single leap. Wilhelm was the first to pound with both fists on the front door.

In the dining room of Mrs. Stolz' boardinghouse, breakfast was nearly finished when she and her boarders heard a commotion on the front porch and urgent knocking on the front door. Mrs. Stolz froze momentarily, frightened her illegal work to save Africans from slavery had been discovered. The loudness, the earnestness of the sounds indicated to her an official inquiry from the police. She rose with dignified resolve to answer the front door, but Carl motioned for her to stay back as he quickly strode down the front hallway to investigate what could be a serious disturbance. He opened the boardinghouse door to an unlikely sight. After months of striving for this moment, and giving up all but a slender shred of hope, the Tangeman brothers found each other. And tears flowed down the cheeks of the brother George and Wilhelm had never seen cry.

Later, when Carl remembered his reunion with George and Wilhelm, he recalled *Isaiah's* (43:2) words:

"When you go through deep waters, I will be with you. When you go through rivers of difficulty, you will not drown."

Epilogue

Carl, Wilhelm and George Tangeman lived in Cincinnati, Ohio for a few years after their reunion. Carl and Wilhelm married the Schiedt sisters: Maria Barbara (Anna Barbara) and Margeretha, respectively. These two brothers fulfilled their dreams to be farmers in locations northeast of Columbus, Ohio including Loudenville, Ashland and Hayesville. Carl and Anna Barbara were the parents of nine children, while Wilhelm and Margeretha had eight children.

George married Sophie Elizabeth Hellmers in Cincinnati where they lived out their lives with their two children.

From 1879 through 1880, Carl, Wilhelm and their families moved to Harvey County, Kansas and purchased land, some of which is still owned and farmed by descendents of Carl and Anna Barbara Schiedt Tangeman.

Family of Carl Heinrich and Anna Barbara Scheidt Tangeman circa 1880.

Anna Elizabeth   Matilda   Gottlob D.   August   Henry W.   John
Eliza   Anna Barbara (Mother) Carl Henry (Father) Paul George   Fred

Glossary

a cappella	Singing without instrumental accompaniment
Alto	Stop
Apfelkuchen	Apple cake
Aqueduct	Overhead waterway used to convey water vessels over land
Auf Wiedersehen	Goodbye
Bahnhof	Train station
Biergarten	German tavern
Bight	Arc
Bitte	Please
Buttermilchsuppe mit speck und zwiebeln	Buttermilk soup with bacon and onions

Christkindl markt	Group of stalls selling Christmas ornaments, handmade gifts and refreshments during the Christmas season
Conscripted	Forced by law to serve in the military forces
Danke	Thanks
Danke schöen	Thank you very much
Emigrant	Person leaving his country of origin
Frau	Mrs.
Frohe Weihnachten	Merry Christmas
Gluhwein	Mulled wine
Guten morgan	Good morning
Guten abend	Good evening
Haus	House
Hawser	A thick rope or cable for mooring or towing a ship
Herr	Mr.
Immigrant	Person arriving in a new country
Ja	Yes
Kinder	Child

Kirche	Church
Lake steamer	Lake vessel powered by steam to transport goods and people across large lakes such as the Great Lakes
Landwehr	Standing army
Lebkuchen	Spicy cookie
Lederstiefel	Boots
Nativists	Local citizens who believe their jobs are threatened by immigrants willing to work for lower wages.
Packet ship	Vessels used for regular transport of mail, freight and passengers between European countries and colonies, North American rivers and canals
Quarantine	Isolation to prevent spread of a contagious disease
Rathaus	Town Hall
Revolution	The forcible overthrow of a government or social order in favor of a new system of governance
River steamer	River vessel powered by steam to transport goods and people up and down rivers
Sandstrom	Local militia
Sauerbraten	Beef roasted with spices

Sauerkraut	Pickled cabbage
Sehr gut	Very good
Shipping agent	Individual whose job it was to recruit passengers from European towns and villages for the packet trade, especially the return voyage from Liverpool to America
Shipping trunk	Sturdy wooden box with handles used to transport goods
slunken	Danish for empty stomach, lean, lank
Spätzle	Dumpling
Sprechen sie Deutsch?	Do you speak German?
Strahlend	Radiant
Wiener schnitzel	Fried pork cutlet

Documented Historical Events

Immigrant in Peril: Carl Tangeman's Heroic Journey, 1847-1848, was inspired by the life of Carl Heinrich Tangeman, 1821-1899. He crossed the Atlantic Ocean from his home in Sulingen, Hannover, Prussia to America in 1847. Although this is a work of historical fiction, the following events are authentic as documented in *The Carl Heinrich Tangeman Genealogy, 1821-1971,* and other sources.

Carl Heinrich Tangeman's birth and death dates and places	CHT Genealogy
Carl Heinrich Tangeman's brothers, sisters and parents	"
Carl Heinrich Tangeman's military service in the Prussian Army	"
The letter from Carl's father, Friedrich Tangeman, to Carl and Elizabeth in c/o Herr Weber in Brake on the Weser River	"
Carl's and Elizabeth's Departure from Bremerhaven, Prussia	"

Deaths of Elizabeth, Dorothee   CHT Genealogy
    and David Tangeman
Collision of the *Talisman* and   Lloyd's Steamboat Directory
    Tempest river steamers,
    November 19, 1847
Flooding on the Ohio River,   Wikipedia
    December, 1847
Account of Carl learning of Wilhelm   CHT Genealogy
    and George's departure to Ohio
    from a parishioner in a
    New York church
Settlement of George, Wilhelm and   Ancestry.com
    Carl Tangeman in Ohio, 1849-1853

Acknowledgements

Immigrant in Peril, a work of historical fiction, is inspired by the genealogical record found in *The Carl Heinrich Tangeman Genealogy, 1821-1971*, compiled by Peg Tangeman Wickersham, Historian for the Tangeman family, and published in 1971. *Immigrant in Peril* would not have been possible without her work to compile the written passages, photos and historical documents into the family genealogy. I am deeply grateful for Peg's genealogical work, her support and encouragement throughout this project.

Of the many friends, family and associates who contributed to this work, I am especially grateful to my husband, Jim Clay, for his encouragement and thoughtful suggestions, my sister, Janice Schroeder for sharing relevant books and her constant support, my children, Paul Clay and Beth Cukier for their interest and feedback, and Wolf, Maren, Ephram, Heidi, Noa and Fred for their enthusiastic questions. Thanks to numerous other individuals who inspired and helped me to complete this book: Dave Chamberlain, Shaila Van Sickle, Linda Simmons, Jane Pearson, Connie Chamberlain, Judy Entz, Jim L. Friesen, John Dustin, and Steve Tangeman.

For readers who desire to learn more about life in the mid-19th century in Europe and the United States and the immigrant experience at that time, I suggest these sources:

Allegheny Portage Railroad. Pennsylvania Historical and Museum Commission. Retrieved from portal.state.pa.us

Carter, H. (Ed.) (1996). *The Past as Prelude: New Orleans, 1718-1968*. Gretna, Louisiana: Pelican Publishing Company, Inc., 1000 Burmaster Street.

Channing, E. (1921). *A History of the United States: The period of transition, 1815-1848*. New York: Macmillan, Publisher.

Cummins, S. (1847). *The Western Pilot, Revised and Corrected by Capts. Chas. Ross and Jno. Klinefelter*. Cincinnati: George Conclin, No. 39, Main Street.

Duffy, J. (Ed.) (1962). *Rudolph Matas History of Medicine in Louisiana*. Binghamton, NY: Vail-Ballou Press, Inc.

Finch, R. G. (1925). *The Story of the New York State Canals Historical and Commercial Information*. State of New York: State Engineer and Surveyor.

Hallett, M. & Karasek, B. (Eds.) (1996). *Folk & Fairy Tales* (2nd ed). Peterborough, Ontario: Broadview Press.

Kamphoefner, W. D., Helbich, W. and Sommer, U. (Eds.) (1991). *News from the Land of Freedom: German Immigrants Write Home*. Ithica, NY: Cornell University Press, 1991.

Lloyd's Steamboat Directory and Disasters on the Western Waters. (1856). Cincinnati, Ohio: James T. Lloyd & Co.

A New Map of Ohio with its Canals Roads & Distances. (1846). Philadelphia: S. Augustus Mitchell, N. E. Corner of Market & 7th Streets.

Shank, W. H. (1986). *The Amazing Pennsylvania Canals, 150th Anniversary Edition*. York, Pennsylvania: American Canal and Transportation Center.

A Twenty-First Century History of the 1847 Kentucky Raid. (2010). Kalamazoo, MI: Fortitude Graphic Design and Publishing.